ANOREXIA NERVOSA

Finding the life line

ANOREXIA NERVOSA

Finding the life line

PATRICIA M. STEIN R.D.,M.S.,M.A. & BARBARA C. UNELL

CompCare®
publications
2415 Annapolis Lane, Minneapolis, Minnesota 55441

Stein, Patricia M., 1935–
 Anorexia nervosa.

 Bibliography: p.
 1. Anorexia nervosa.   I. Unell, Barbara,
1951–   . II. Title.
RC552.A5S78 1985   616.85'2   85-26889
ISBN 0-89638-084-X

Cover design by Jeremy Gale
Cover photograph by Jim Arndt Photography

 Inquiries, orders, and catalog requests should be addressed to
 CompCare Publications
 2415 Annapolis Lane
 Minneapolis, Minnesota 55441
 Call toll free 800/328-3330
 (Minnesota residents 559-4800)

 2   3   4   5   6
86   87   88   89   90

Those of us who can claim to be cured of anorexia nervosa know that somewhere along the way our base human instinct to survive took over. In my case, it was a matter of learning to be imperfect, to accept that I am prone to the same levels of failure and success as anyone else . . . Years of therapy, and years of patience on the part of my husband and family gave me the confidence to accept what I saw in the mirror.

"Mirror, Mirror" by Deborah Gelbach, *Twin Cities*, October 1984

A new perspective on anorexia

Many articles and books have appeared about anorexia nervosa by therapists and researchers. Our primary purpose in this book is to offer information about this condition of self-starvation from another point of view—that of recovering anorexics.

We interviewed recovering persons, asking them about their experiences before they discovered they had anorexia, how their disorder progressed, what kind of treatment they had undergone, if any, and what they felt was most helpful in overcoming the problem.

All responded voluntarily to our requests for interviewees placed through therapists and other medical professionals.

All except one were women. This is not unusual, since an estimated 85 to 95 percent of anorexics are women. They came from different backgrounds, were at different ages when they experienced anorexia, and recovered over varying periods of time. One developed the syndrome more than thirteen years ago and has known several years of recovery. One had only a few months of recovery at the time of our interview. In all cases, names, places, and other details have been changed to assure their anonymity.

Although anorexia nervosa is sometimes seen with symptoms of another disorder, bulimia (victims alternately binge and starve or binge and purge through self-induced vomiting and often through the use of laxatives and diuretics), most interviewed here were "primary anorexics" or "restrictive anorexics." That is, they controlled weight through limiting their caloric intake and sometimes also through excessive exercise. The male anorexic and three of the women showed bulimic symptoms as well; their experience included food-bingeing as well as food-restricting.

The *Diagnostic Statistical Manual of Mental Disorders* (also known as the *DSM III*) describes anorexia and bulimia as separate disorders, but more than one researcher has suggested that they may be stages on the same continuum. In any case, the crossover between the two disorders is not unusual. In fact, approximately one fourth of those with anorexia also show symptoms of bulimia. Some estimates are higher.

This is a book of hope, although the life stories it tells are sometimes dark and frightening. Since anorexia nervosa is a complex disorder and there may be a tendency to oversimplify the "answers"—especially in retrospect, those interviewed felt strongly that they did not want to be cast as role models or advisors. However they were hopeful that their candid experiences might offer some clues to prevention, treatment, and recovery. Through telling about what seemed to work to bring about recovery, each person could show how she or he perceived that the problem was overcome.

Most important of all, these life stories demonstrate that recovery is possible; individuals who experience anorexia can—and usually do—go on to lead positive and productive lives.

Our wish is that anorexics or persons at risk of developing anorexia, as well as families and friends who perhaps are unaware that someone they love may be struggling with this disorder, can be helped to recognize the symptoms by reading this book. Also, we hope that individuals who suspect they have anorexia and are afraid or ashamed to ask for help may be motivated to do so after seeing themselves mirrored in these experiences.

The interviews in Part One are followed by supplementary informational chapters in Part Two. Part Two includes perspectives on anorexia nervosa by medical professionals, as well as summaries comparing the anorexics' stories and relating the disorder to increasing societal pressures to be thin.

Although background information is included, this book does not attempt to be either a scientific report or a thorough presentation of current theories about causes, symptoms, and treatment of anorexia nervosa. Instead, it is a vehicle for anorexics to tell in their own words how they lived for a time as shadows of themselves, and how they found a way out of their self-destructive obsessions.

For our mothers, Louise McConnaughey Gardner Meierhoff
and Josephine B. Coleman.

We wish to express our appreciation to those who share their experiences here, for their belief in this book and their willingness to help others in the struggle against anorexia nervosa.

Thanks, too, to Barbara P. Lukert, M.D., and Frederick S. Mittleman, M.D., who gave time and expertise to expand the scope of the information included here; to our editors, Jane Thomas Noland, Leslie Reindl, and Susan Van Pelt; and to Denise C. Perkins, M.A., a treatment professional who served as content consultant.

We owe a special debt of gratitude to our typists, Doris Eichenwald, Diana Middleton, and Mary P. Wharton, and to our husbands, Ira Stein and Robert Unell, for their encouragement and support.

Contents

Part One
In their own words

Laura M.

Laura credits her turn away from anorexia nervosa to her feelings of thankfulness for being alive after a near-fatal illness—and to finding a sympathetic friend. Her illness showed her there was something more important in life than what she was or was not going to eat.

What was your life like as a child in Iowa?

Not very pleasant. Lonely. In fact, it was really dull. You could say I was a loner and food was the highlight of my life. I was always a little plumper and more weight-conscious than others, with not much social life. In fact, I didn't even date until I was eighteen and in college. My family had no social outlet except for occasional visits with relatives. We didn't vacation or attend church activities. The important thing for my parents was that I got good grades, so my life focused on schoolwork. I didn't participate in any of the "fun" social events at school. There was TV, schoolwork—and food.

Did you have negative encounters with your parents over food?

Cooking made my mom feel good. She would cook and I would eat. My dad would always get after me just as I was sticking some fattening food into my mouth. I remember he said once as I was eating a big piece of chocolate cake, "One of these days you'll regret that piece of cake. The boys won't want you when you're big and fat."

What was your dad like?

He was an authoritarian. There was no rebelling against my father. I knew that, so I didn't ask to do anything special. I knew the answer before asking. Often I'd hear my dad arguing with my mom. He'd

1

always say, "When the kids get grown, I'm going to leave." Sure enough, when I went off to college, he did. My mom always said I had my father wrapped around my little finger, but I was not aware of that. He was never affectionate with me.

When did your weight become an issue for you?

When I was twelve or thirteen I began trying to diet because I considered myself chunkier than a lot of the kids. I would go on diets with my mom.

Later, when I got married, I gained weight. I was nineteen and weighed about 124 pounds then. I played the traditional role of caring and cooking for my husband, whom I idolized. In turn, he took great pleasure in opening up my sheltered life after all those years of never going out even to eat, to a movie, to a dance.

When I learned I couldn't get pregnant, I turned to food for comfort from the pain of this news. Also, food became a communication bond between my mom and me. "I've just taken an apple pie out of the oven," Mom would call and say. "Come on over with the kids" (we'd adopted two). And I'd pack up the kids and go.

My husband was transferred and we moved to St. Louis. There I was with two kids, no friends, and a husband who traveled more than he was at home. I was so lonely. My work was my house.

I weighed 112 when we moved, but I cooked and ate myself up to 148 pounds and a size fourteen pants. I hated both the pounds and the pants.

I remember the day I started my diet, the diet that led me down the anorexia road. I tried on my size fourteen pants and asked my husband, "Don't you think I'm too heavy?" He replied, "Yeah, you *are* getting big in the rear end." I can tell you the exact day and the year. I was bound and determined to get that weight off.

What was your typical eating and exercise plan?

I ate the same thing every day for six weeks at a time—300 calories a day. I'd have tea for breakfast, with artificial sweetener, and lettuce with a few green beans for lunch. I'd wash the beans so there would be no trace of salt on them; I didn't want to retain any liquid. For dinner I'd have two ounces of broiled meat, squeezed until it was like paper to get rid of the grease, and maybe a couple of bites of lettuce.

I couldn't eat in front of people, never ate with the family. I had to have my own food by myself so I could pick at it. If we went out, sometimes I could eat a lettuce salad, but that was all. If I didn't have *my* food, I wouldn't eat.

I joined a fitness center and went seven days a week, even though I had two small children at home.

What were your husband's and family's reactions to your new diet and exercise program?

In the beginning, my husband was concerned that I was not eating enough. I couldn't wait for him to go out of town so I could eat what I wanted in peace. My kids, three and six years old at the time, just knew that this is the way Mommy ate.

How did you feel about yourself at this time?

I had started other projects in the past and then dropped them when I couldn't do them perfectly. I was so proud of myself and on a "high" because I had finally found something I could do better than anyone else. Everyone I knew complained of failing to lose weight on diets. My doctor later said he didn't know how I had mustered the energy to take care of the house, the kids, and my husband on so little nutrition.

I was oversensitive to touch, cold, noise. I lost lots of hair and my periods stopped. But this was "my thing," and I didn't notice the destruction because I was totally wrapped up in it. I had no friends at all. Losing weight was the focus of my entire world.

How did you learn about anorexia nervosa?

I had never read anything about anorexia nervosa. My husband was appalled by my behavior and confused by my actions. I had to hide my diet books from him. Then I developed an abnormal vaginal discharge, and my husband convinced me to get help. I checked into a hospital for two days, but I couldn't tolerate the place because they didn't give me "my" plain green beans for food. I was told I had some mental problems, had anorexia nervosa, and should have counseling. My husband pleaded with me to get my weight up to 100 pounds (I weighed 83 at the time).

I got up and walked out of the hospital without the doctor's consent and came home. Being back in the house made me feel secure. I could not stand for my routine to be broken; that would throw me into a panic. Everything I did was perfectly routinized, ritualized. My doctor had told me I was in danger of dying if I left the hospital. I told him I'd die rather than eat. I now see what a serious statement that was when I had a husband and two kids. But I didn't see it then.

What helped you turn away from self-starvation?

My husband's pleading just reinforced my desire to diet, but reading books on the subject of anorexia helped me learn about what I was doing to myself. I'd see me in those books and be amazed that other people knew about my private world.

I saw a therapist six or eight times after leaving the hospital and he suggested that I look for some outside interests. The counseling did not seem to help, though I think it would have if my therapist had known more about anorexia then.

During one of my ten-mile daily walks in my neighborhood, I met a woman my age. She was overweight and I was underweight, but we never discussed our physical size. We became friends, walked and began to bowl together. But it was well over a year after we met that we talked about weight. My diet then consisted of pressure-cooked chicken breast and boiled okra.

Slowly I began to eat a little more, but still couldn't eat with other people. I would, on occasion, succumb to the pressures of others to eat and would actually eat more. I intended to try to break this thing, but each time I changed my food rituals, I would binge, and then I would be right back into starvation. Starvation was the only thing that made me feel secure.

I told my friend I had difficulty with food. She never said, "Why don't you gain weight?" That's why I trusted her. She was someone I could talk to and she would listen to me. Her friendship was one of the things that helped me most. She never offered advice or suggestions, never pressured me the way my mom and my husband did. Most important, she didn't judge me. She just listened and accepted me for myself. Before this friendship developed, I felt I had nothing except my house. Although I loved the kids and my husband, even they were not as important to me as my diet. My diet was *it!* I'm bothered by saying that now, but at the time that's the way it was.

When did you decide to eat more?

It was gradual. The kids would say, "Mama, would you please eat with us tonight?" I began on my own to make the decision to eat more, after the hospital experience and the therapist's suggestion to get involved in outside interests. I had setbacks, but I kept trying to break out of the pattern during a span of six or seven years by praying for help to overcome the problem. The decision to eat was my own. I got up to 95 pounds and promised myself that I would change. My family became more important to me.

Besides my good friend, I met another woman as I was walking. I could tell she was anorexic, and we became friends. It was reassuring to meet someone with the same disease. I had felt for so long I was the only one in the world with this problem.

Would you describe your illness?

I used enemas, diuretics, and laxatives, but basically I depended on food restriction and exercise. I always felt as if I was in control, when actually it was the other way around—my obsession with food and weight was controlling me!

What was your life like after you made the decision to eat more?

I still feared weighing over 100 pounds. When my weight finally got over that mark, I realized that food really was not poison to me after all. Some interest in food came back. But I told myself that 105 was the maximum for me (I'm five feet three inches tall).

Have there been any major changes in your life since then?

Last winter I was severely ill. I had diarrhea for three months, but secretly I was happy about it because I was getting rid of the food and staying at 105 pounds. I was hospitalized for eighteen days with an abcessed appendix, anemia, and dehydration. When I finally came home, I was so thankful to be alive that food and diet didn't hold so much importance for me. I decided I wanted to live. My doctor told me that I must eat so that my body could repair itself. And I did eat. Gradually I started gaining weight and getting involved with other interests—the family, what the kids were doing, and so on.

How do you feel today about yourself, your weight, and your problem of anorexia?

It's been seven years since the onset of anorexia nervosa. Today I weigh 132 pounds, which I believe is too heavy for me, but I don't feel strongly enough about it to cut back again. I am enjoying foods I haven't had in ten years. In fact, I can't seem to get enough of the foods I love. I gained this weight on food I really wanted to eat, like bagels and chocolate chip cookies.

Thoughts do creep back; occasionally I think about dieting and exercising excessively again, but when I do cut calories and do my walking, it is in moderation. I will *not* have anorexia again.

People with my kind of compulsive personality have to watch out. I feel that anorexics are never cured; they just learn how to control their situation and keep the disease within bounds. Food and weight always are going to be issues with me, I think. I don't weigh food now, but I do count calories; I can figure them mentally.

I'm thirty-four years old. I tell myself I'm not eighteen any more, and I don't have to have a model's figure. It's more important to me that my kids think I'm normal. I want to eat that birthday cake!

How have your eating habits changed?

Before, I ate alone, and if I ate one thing that was off my list, I'd binge and then fast for three or four days. Now I have no list. I usually eat with my family, and I eat some of everything. I am still fearful of eating too much, though, because the more I eat, the more I want to eat.

What are your personal goals?

To eat what I want to eat. I've met two of my goals already—not weighing every day and enjoying life!

Heather T.

Heather hated what she saw in herself when she reached her lowest weight, yet at five feet seven inches and 90 pounds she felt overweight. She stopped starving herself when a medical professional convinced her that she needed to gain weight to restore her ability to think and carry on her art work.

How would you describe your eating habits as a child?

Our home was a sugar-lover's dream come true. Two or three coffee cakes always lay waiting in the kitchen freezer. My mom would make fresh cookies every Saturday morning. I now know that I still connect a coffee cake, brownies, or cookies with my mother's caring for my sister and me.

I remember only one negative experience about food at home. I wanted two hamburgers for dinner and my mom said, "No, I think you'd better just stop right there." That was the only time I can remember her ever saying no to me when I really wanted something, particularly something to eat.

When did you first become conscious of your weight?

My high school years basically were happy, but my spirits sank to great depths of despair when shorts-and-swimming-suit weather appeared. My body just did not seem to match my friends' bodies. I was the only one—or so it seemed to me—with a big, flabby tummy and thighs and squishy upper arms. Twiggy was "in" at the time, and I was constantly wishing I could have her shape. I thought all my friends looked like her and that I was heavy in comparison. I weighed about 110 pounds and was five feet seven inches tall. I was not well versed in how to go about dieting, since no emphasis ever was placed on cutting down on food at home.

When I began college, I did not concern myself with my weight. I was having a terrific time academically and socially. I discovered such delights as the pop machine at the dorm that gave you as much soft drink as you liked whenever you wanted it. I ate and drank what I pleased, as did most of my new college friends.

When I came home for vacation and visited friends at the place where I had worked, they all joked about my "ballooned" body. (I'd gained twenty pounds.) Their comments burst my happy, self-assured bubble. I vowed to eat less, and I did lose the weight that following summer.

The next year I alternately binged and starved until I became so hung up on food that what I ate would make or break my day.

Did anyone know about your food habits?

I told no one. I had several heavy-eating, overeating friends who thought nothing of our starving and bingeing. I kept my shame, guilt, and anxiety inside. I made great grades, dated a lot, and enjoyed my college years socially.

Then I met Mr. Wonderful, and my crazy eating habits stopped. Love seemed to satisfy my every need. I ate normally until after graduation.

When did your serious symptoms of anorexia begin?

The day after I graduated from college. I suddenly admitted to myself that I had no idea what to do with my life, no real goal for what I wanted to be when I "grew up." I was confused and scared, but I didn't know how to help myself. My parents always had made decisions for me. They gave me no responsibility at home, and I simply had never thought that I would someday have to plan my adult life on my own.

I knew my parents expected me to get a job, but all of a sudden a job wasn't enough. With no personal direction, I was miserable and didn't know why. I had always been so "together." Now, at twenty-three, I thought I was losing my mind, but I didn't share my feelings with anyone.

I started practicing unhealthy eating habits again, as I'd done during college. I would go without eating and then would eat a lot of one thing.

I broke off my relationship with my boyfriend, thinking that standing back from this relationship would help me sort out my confusion. I agonized over leaving the person I truly loved; I now know how deeply guilty I felt for leaving him—and how confused about not being able to sort out or explain to him my feelings so he could help me.

I didn't intentionally begin to starve myself: I was so distraught emotionally that I got physically sick when I ate. My weight began to drop. My friends' positive feedback about my weight loss was just what I needed then, when I felt so bad about myself. I thought losing weight was great because finally I was as slim as I thought my high school buddies had been.

I kept eating less and less until the size fives finally fit! I was not aware I had a problem; I was not able to think rationally because of the starvation. I could accomplish nothing at my weight of ninety pounds. My mind was totally obsessed with food, but I still could not explain my feelings to anyone.

How did you feel about yourself then?

I had always thought that if I were ever thin, really thin, the world would be mine. Now at less than 90 pounds, I still saw myself as not thin enough. I was unaware of how thin I looked until one day when I was riding a bicycle in my bathing suit, someone yelled from a passing car, "Hey, skeleton!" I thought, "Could that be me?" No one had ever encouraged *me* to gain weight! I was incredulous. My friends and family always gave my weight loss positive reinforcement with comments like, "Wow, you've really gotten trim!"

I couldn't eat with friends, couldn't eat bread, sweets, or other starches. I was having headaches and was extremely nervous and sensitive to others. I began to realize I had a problem but didn't know its name. The "skeleton" label hurt, just as the "fatso" barbs had a few years before. Even though I was a different person from the one I used to be, I liked myself no better now.

Was this when you realized you needed help?

I'm still amazed that hearing guys my age, total strangers, call me "skeleton" caused me to go see a doctor. My thinking was so muddled. My periods had stopped, so I went to a gynecologist to see what was wrong. Never mentioning anorexia nervosa, he told me that I was in premature menopause, that I would never have children and should take drugs to keep my system from aging.

Luckily, I could not accept this diagnosis, so I went to see an internist. He also never brought up anorexia nervosa, but told me that if

I remained at my low current weight of 90 pounds, my liver, my heart, my mental and physical health in general would be destroyed. Until then I had never connected my starving myself with my headaches or my confused emotional state.

Later I learned that my internist was also a psychiatrist; I saw him regularly for about six months for what I thought were physical problems only. During this time he insisted I gain weight or he would have to hospitalize me. Our discussions dealt only with food and gaining weight.

Because of his threat of hospitalization, I began to eat more. Slowly I found that I could make decisions. I learned how helpful it was, mentally and emotionally, to express my feelings, which up to now I had never done, not with my family, my friends, or my peers at work. Gradually I recognized that I *did* have feelings, thoughts, and desires that seemed to interest others—goals and dreams that I needed to follow. Also I learned to accept others' comments without being defensive.

I could not believe how this nightmare of compulsive dieting, as yet unnamed for me even by my doctors, had taken control of my life and masked the "real" problem. I never saw myself as dangerously thin. I thought I looked great at 90 pounds, horrible at 100, and even worse at 110, the weight I maintained until last year, when my first child was born.

Were your visits with your doctor the catalyst
for your overcoming anorexia?

The self-starvation ended there, but some conflicts remained unresolved for nearly seven years until they were finally brought to the surface through counseling with a different therapist.

What did your experience with anorexia nervosa teach you?

I realize that sixteen-to-twenty-year-olds who are trying to establish their break from parental controls need support and guidance in that separation, especially if they have been dominated by protective, albeit loving, parents.

Starving oneself, overeating, using drugs, or clinging to a cult is often a way of avoiding thinking for oneself about the future or about who and what one really is inside. Without friends to talk to, without self-awareness, without plans for adulthood, the transition to independence may be filled with destruction instead of hope.

Growing up is painful. Having some self-confidence, self-control, and self-esteem is crucial to easing the pain.

Sarah W.

Wanting to conceive and have a healthy baby gave Sarah the motivation to begin to gain weight after losing over twenty-five pounds with anorexia nervosa. In her own eyes, the real turning point in overcoming anorexia came when she began a new job at what she perceived as her "high weight." She discovered that she could make friends easily and realized that her weight was unimportant to others. For the first time, she felt accepted.

How did you feel about yourself when you were young?

I always wanted to lose a few pounds. As a child, I saw myself as ugly and fat, not "bright, wonderful, and terrific" as my mother described me. Mom was a gourmet cook, overweight, and an alcoholic. I spent my whole childhood trying to believe what my mother always said about me, but I couldn't.

Mother had her own vision of me and the world, a romantic vision that was out of step with the reality I perceived. My perception of our family and the family dynamics were not the same as her rosy, pretty world, so I tended to discount the positive things she would tell me.

I felt scared and unsure of myself, so I put on an act of being cold and distant. Guys thought I was aloof, but I had girlfriends. My mom was so charming; I knew my friends often came over just to see her.

I know she never meant to cause me any harm, but I now feel that her care for me when I was a child was inconsistent, and that this inconsistency had a lot to do with my emotional upheaval then and later in life. The inconsistency must have been due, in part, to the alcoholism and to financial pressures and tensions in our family relationships.

My mother's two sons by her former husband lived with us from time to time, and I think my mom never got over the idea that she had abandoned them. My younger brother started doing drugs when he was eleven or twelve years old.

When did your weight and thinness become important to you?

I never really had been away from home before I went away to college. My weight was average at the time. During my first year at college, I began to eat less—because the food was so bad, I told myself. Actually, I had a six-foot-tall, knockout, fun-loving roommate who looked gorgeous to me. She was always on a "diet," and somehow her concern with dieting just filtered down to me, though I never called my eating less and less a "diet."

During the days, I lived on cottage cheese and salad and diet pop. Then at night I ate popcorn and went on uncontrollable binges. I didn't even know the word "binge" then, but I'd think it was just awful that I couldn't control my eating at midnight the way I could in the daytime.

My mother noticed my gradual weight loss throughout my years at college, but nevered bothered me about it. I was getting only positive feedback from men, having a good time, and feeling better about my intelligence because of good grades. Then, at the age of nineteen, my periods stopped, and that worried me.

Had you heard of anorexia nervosa?

Thirteen years ago, in the early 1970s, I'd never heard of it. I'd undergone extensive medical testing because of missing periods. I even had exploratory surgery. But no medical person ever mentioned anorexia nervosa. One doctor's treatment suggestion was, "Go eat a hamburger." And he was serious!

What happened after this?

I was married at twenty-one and after that I ate less and less. My weight was probably around 110 pounds and I'm five feet five and a half inches tall. I can remember reasoning that people always get fatter after they get married, so I wanted to start off thin. I kept up my bingeing at night, but never took laxatives or diuretics or forced myself to vomit.

I brushed my teeth compulsively. Eventually, I got so I'd have nothing but diet pop during the day, and I chewed gum a lot. For dinner I'd have a salad with my husband. Later at night I'd have puffed wheat because I could eat a lot of it but take in few calories.

14

The bingeing scared my husband. He thought something was wrong and made me consult a psychologist. I was just a mess. For the next two years I saw this therapist twice a week for what was termed depression. I had a severe problem with my self-image, paired with constant insomnia. I always felt uncomfortable around other people—I thought they were watching me critically. The psychologist tried to help me build up my self-image.

About a year and a half into this therapy, I was hospitalized for being suicidal and severely depressed. My brother had died in January the year before from drug-related causes, and my mother had died the following May of liver failure due to her alcoholism. During this first hospitalization—one year after my mother's death—I stayed only a week, then went back a few weeks later for what they called a grief reaction. I weighed 110 pounds.

At first the hospital staff members were more concerned about my depression than about my weight. I now know that my therapist thought I should feel in control of my life and didn't consider my low weight to be life-threatening. I suspect he probably told the staff not to push food on me. I was in heaven; they didn't try to make me eat! Finally, however, they noticed I was losing weight and told me that if I didn't start eating I'd die. This made me more depressed than ever because I thought I had found a place where I didn't have to eat—or even get out of bed—and now they were screwing things up!

After I passed out one day, they changed their treatment. My weight was down to 95 pounds. They force-fed me by tube, and that was the worst experience of all, the most painful, the most humiliating and degrading. I cried and argued and cut myself with razor blades, stood under hot showers, did anything I could to inflict pain on myself. I was taking out on my own body my anger and frustration at those who were making me eat.

When I was released after four months, the maximum time I could spend in the hospital, the doctors told me I had anorexia nervosa. After another two months of severe depression and more weight loss—I weighed 90 pounds now—I decided I wanted a baby. My husband, however, decided I should go back into the hospital. He was more concerned that I might kill myself than he was about my weight. So I went back for another month or more. I was really depressed because I wanted a baby. I was told I had a depressive personality. Today I know that is not true, but that was the diagnosis at the time.

What do you feel helped you the most?

Well, the hospitalizations kept me alive at a time when I was very suicidal. And my psychologist was wonderful; he didn't always know the right thing to do, but I knew he cared. Probably one of the most important events of my life was having a child. Although pregnancy and parenthood obviously are not "cures" for anorexia, getting pregnant and having a healthy baby became a priority in my life at this time. I took Pergonal [a drug to stimulate ovulation—Ed.] in order to conceive. It worked, even though my weight was only 98 pounds at the time of conception. My first child was born a year after my third hospitalization. During pregnancy I could eat because I was doing it for someone else; I had a real responsibility. I gained nineteen pounds while pregnant—and I felt wonderful.

What was your life like after your child was born?

Six or seven months after the baby came, my milk dried up. I went back to eating "funny." I took Valium [a commonly used prescription tranquilizer—Ed.], and my weight dropped to 75 pounds. I was still seeing the same psychologist three times a week, and he and my friends were appalled. I never saw it. I thought it was thrilling that I was losing weight. My therapist had a nurse come to my house and review my intake several times a week. We would spend two hours planning a day's menu of 500 calories. We became great friends. I was obsessed with food, with cooking, with cookbooks. Today I know that this was the wrong approach—to focus on the food—but my therapist, I feel, did the best he knew how to do at the time.

We then moved to Cincinnati. I weighed 80 pounds. Because I decided I wanted another baby, I began eating, slowly. Right after we moved, I started seeing a psychiatrist, who told me he couldn't be responsible for my health, "if you don't start eating a normal diet." Seven or eight months later, I weighed 115 and felt grotesque. I was very depressed about this weight gain; I can't even explain *how* I gained!

It was then I went voluntarily to a private mental hospital, where I stayed for two months. Before I went in, I was yelling and screaming and taking overdoses of Valium. My husband and I were not getting along. I thought he hated me because I was so heavy and ugly.

The doctors there recommended that I be hospitalized for an indefinite period; they said it might take years for me to get well. They told me I had an anorexic personality and anorexic tendencies. I think if I'd been covered by an insurance plan that would have paid for the hospitalization I would have consented to stay there. I didn't, so they suggested I go to a local hospital for inpatient treatment. I walked through the place and knew there was no way I would stay there, so I enrolled in their outpatient therapy sessions. I thought I was trying to lose weight, but I was still bingeing frequently. My weight did not drop. In fact, I now weighed 140 pounds, and I felt I had to hide. I was worried I'd see someone I knew, so I'd go out of my way to get to the grocery store and other places. I existed only for my child.

What finally turned things around for you?

The job I got at an insurance company was an important milestone in my recovery. I realized through my job that I could exist in the world at what I thought was a too-heavy weight—that people could respond favorably to me the way I was. They accepted me for *me*. Since I was good at my job, I got a lot of positive feedback. For the first time, I realized my weight was unimportant to people.

Suddenly my periods came back. I was afraid that they would go away again if I dieted. I wanted another child, and I was thirty-one. I would have done almost anything to have another baby. After twelve years of all the counseling, all the problems, gradually I started feeling better about myself and seeing friends. The cumulative effect of the therapy I'd had over the years helped me be more comfortable with myself. Things finally came together for me.

On a trip to Chicago, my husband and I took time to get to know each other again. We became very close once more and decided to have another baby. We did. And the twenty pounds I gained during my second pregnancy is still on me!

Today I'd like to lose weight, but mostly I would like to eat normally. The past isn't as hard to talk about now. I just need to go on with my life, knowing this fact about myself—that for all these years I have been fighting a disease, the disease of anorexia nervosa.

Erin P.

When a psychologist helped her begin to see herself as an individual needing and deserving a self-fulfilling life of her own, Erin began to turn away from self-starvation. In the process of looking inside herself for beauty and self-worth, she discovered her own spirituality. She learned to notice more than the outside appearance of people—including herself—and to appreciate these inner qualities.

How would you describe your childhood?

I remember my childhood as a very happy, very loving time. My parents were demonstrative, verbally and physically, in their affection. I was born with a deformed leg, and my parents were told I would never walk at all. So they would just put me down someplace, and I would stay. I was a quiet, passive, good little girl for the first years of my life and remained so, even after I began to walk at about age three.

As I look back, I would say my parents were quite protective. I had continuous health problems as a child; for instance, my eardrums kept bursting from infections during my kindergarten year. But the issue of weight did not come up until I was a sophomore in high school.

Was food a subject of talk around the house when you were growing up?

My mom was a professional model, and she always had me on a diet to lose weight in high school—"to look good." When I gained twenty pounds one summer, that was it for my parents—no more overweight for me! I went on a diet, and for the rest of high school, my life focused on weight, diets, and exercise. In spite of all the emphasis on dieting, I ate all the junk food everyone my age did, even though my mom would give me trouble about it. I enjoyed eating. The fact that I'd lost my sense of smell in an accident at age six didn't seem to affect my appetite. I never felt at the time that I was hung up on food.

How did this focus on appearance affect the way you felt about yourself?

Since I looked like my father, I felt sure I did not have the radiant beauty of my mother. My three brothers looked like my mom and also modeled. My constant comparing myself with my mother reflected my general lack of self-esteem.

One important emotional outlet was my involvement with the theater beginning in junior and senior high school. I could play parts and be somebody other than myself.

What triggered your severe weight loss —the diets your mother imposed on you?

No. On her diets, I would lose weight and then regain it. After I was married, I got down to 105 pounds (I am five feet six inches tall), not by consciously eating less, really. The weight just starting falling off. I was on a birth control pill for three years and during this time my periods kept gradually decreasing in volume and duration. Then they stopped completely. Mom started giving me articles about anorexia to read.

After my periods stopped, I went to see a doctor. His solution was to take me off that particular pill. He blamed my weight loss on the pill. He was concerned about my reproductive system, not my weight loss. He never mentioned the words "anorexia nervosa."

I went to see another doctor, who put me on Provera [a derivative of progesterone used sometimes to stimulate the return of menstrual periods—Ed.]. I had one period and got pregnant. After the birth of my child, my doctor prescribed another pill, assuring me that this milder birth control pill would not affect my menstrual cycle the way the other had.

How did weight loss affect your eating habits? What happened after the pill change?

I ate a normal pregnancy diet. Then, after my first child was born, I had a terrible flu and lost my appetite. After that, the habit of not eating just stuck. I also seemed to lose weight on the new pill just as I had on the other one. My periods slowed down and stopped again.

My husband traveled a great deal, and while he was gone I didn't eat much. I'd exist on some fruit and cottage cheese. This went on for several years.

My mom and my husband were the only family members who ever said anything about my weight; I'd let their comments go in one ear and out the other. I thought they were crazy. I didn't think there was a thing wrong with me or the way I ate. Every time I'd see my parents, the subject of food turned into a big thing with my mother. For example, when she came over for my birthday dinner once, she started crying because I was so thin. I hated seeing her upset. I could see I was thin, all right, but I liked what I saw.

How did your friends react to your weight loss?

Some of them kept telling me to eat and would literally stuff food into my mouth at parties. I just thought they were being rude. You see, I have a stubborn streak. I knew if I ate more, I would be doing it to please them, rather than myself.

When did you start hearing someone's concern about you?

Two years ago I heard a psychologist speak at church. He was a beautiful person, and I felt he was someone I could talk with, that he could help me work out the negative feelings I had toward myself.

I was becoming aware that I needed to make some changes in my self-image. So I called him and he talked to me at great length on the telephone, "as long as I wanted to talk," as he said. We didn't discuss weight, just self-image. He told me that I should call him when I was ready to make the first appointment.

I don't know why, but I suddenly decided to take the first step, to find out what was going on with me. I felt I needed to change my attitude about life and find out who I was. I needed to see if it was okay to be me instead of what I perceived others wanted me to be.

I started seeing him and continued working with him for one year, up until a year ago. He never wanted to work on my weight, just on my emotional situation at the time. He didn't talk about my childhood, only about how I felt about myself. Through the course of this year of self-examination, meditation, and the relationship with the therapist, I began to be more sure of myself. Before the therapy, I had ignored the spiritual side of myself. With the therapist's aid, I came to know what

21

was important. Now my spiritual life is paramount to me. It's more than just a belief in God. I now live what I believe. I am being true to myself.

Finally I told him I was ready to stop seeing him, but not before I had decided, with his help, that I could do what I set my mind to. For instance, a year and a half ago I decided I was going to be able to smell, and one morning I bent over a flower and I could smell it! When I decided I was going to add weight, I did it. Slowly. I announced I was going to gain sixteen pounds last year, and I did it on my own, mind over matter.

I put on five pounds one time when I knew I would be going to the beach in a swimming suit. My husband told me people would gawk at me because I was so thin. Gawk? They never even noticed me! I gained that weight to please myself as well as my husband! I definitely feel that if you're going to get over a problem like mine, it must come from your heart, from really wanting to for whatever reason.

What helped you maintain your recovery?

Daily meditations, taking myself away from the outer world, getting away from the physical setup around me. I think you can do anything you want to do and be anything you want to be if you put your mind and heart into it. For example, until last year, I called myself a girl. I never thought of myself as a woman. I had a powerful mother; I know that now in retrospect. I also realized that through all these years I had idolized my husband and never really grown up. Whatever he said, I agreed with. Now my life slowly is becoming more self-fulfilling.

I have realized how hard it is for children to build self-esteem if they can't pick up cues from their mothers, and I'm trying very hard to help my child's self-concept be as strong as it can be by building a strong self-concept for myself too.

Christie F.

Christie suffered from anorexia first at the age of nine and again in her late teens. As a child, she spent a year and a half in a psychiatric treatment facility undergoing intensive therapy. In overcoming the disorder, she credits getting past the powerlessness of childhood and college years, and learning to reach out for support and express her feelings.

How would you describe your life when you first had anorexia?

I am the third child between two older brothers and a younger sister. At the age of nine I felt powerless in my position in the family. Both my parents were very controlling and domineering. The anorexia nervosa was my way of taking some control over my life. Starving myself was a form of manipulation, as well as a way of escaping, a retreat.

Were you hospitalized?

Yes. I was in a local hospital for about two months and then transferred to a psychiatric treatment center facility for a year and a half. This was in the early 1960s, when most professionals didn't know much about anorexia. They were just shooting from the hip in their form of intervention. Now that I know more about therapy myself, I see that they really didn't know any better. I don't hold it against them. In the local hospital, two psychiatrists worked with me. One of them was excellent.

What kinds of therapy were used?

At the psychiatric treatment center, they used a psychoanalytic, Freudian approach. At that time anorexia was thought to be an individual's fear of getting pregnant. And then, of course, they got into my earlier childhood and relationships. The doctors at the local hospital did try to do some explorations of "here and now" issues too.

Was that productive?

They used a pretty intensive approach. Besides seeing a psychiatrist twice a week, I was in a group at the place where I was living. Also, my social workers were always with me. I guess one of the positives was being removed from my home. Whereas today professionals would strongly suggest family therapy, in those days counselors met with parents separately. But even that was helpful because it opened up my parents' views, helped them to be more in touch with what was going on.

Did you actively starve yourself?

Yes. I was already a thin kid and never saw myself as having a weight problem. I never viewed myself as fat when I was anorexic at the age of nine. Food was important at our house, but I don't recall it being an issue. My family was conscious of eating right, of eating well-balanced meals.

After a period of supposed recovery, I had a recurrence of anorexia nervosa during my freshman year in college. I had lost weight in the middle of my junior year in high school, but when I went to college I was starting to put on the pounds. My mom said, "We'll have to put you on a diet." At first I was really rebellious that I had to do that. Then I put myself on a rigid diet and got down to 105 pounds and looked fine. And then my mom said, "You don't want to get any thinner," but I just kept going.

In college I was a pre-med student—just studied all the time and watched my diet and exercised a lot. I didn't do things with other people because I was trying to do well in school. I didn't like the college town; it was very sequestered. I was there for about a year.

Then the college had financial problems, so I came back home. My weight was about 95 pounds. Because I was feeling irritated a lot—had crying bouts and so forth—my doctor tested me for hypoglycemia. I was hypoglycemic, so he put me on a high-protein, high-fat diet and urged me to gain weight. He did not mention anorexia. I worked with two therapists, one who wasn't helpful at all, then with a more effective one for a year and a half.

How did you overcome anorexia the first time?

Very gradually I became aware of the people around me and began reaching out to them, developing support systems. I know there is no way I could physically go through that starvation regimen now. But I don't think anorexics ever lose that obsessive-compulsive part of themselves. Instead they may funnel it into something more socially acceptable.

Now, being on my own, I can steer in the directions I want to go. I'm not tied down because of being a child or a college student. At those times I felt completely powerless. In college, I still wanted to be a child; I didn't want to grow up and deal with my own sexuality. So getting past all that helped me turn away from anorexia nervosa. I became more in touch with my feelings, individuating myself from my family.

What were your feelings about your therapists?

Well, I have some really strong feelings about some of them. I feel they were just keeping me on to get money from me. In looking back at their approach, there was no structure to speak of, no goal-setting, none of that. The therapy consisted of just talking. With the therapist I had in college, the talk was about superficial kinds of things—surface conversation. I remember one time he said, "You sure like to talk." That just blew my mind because I thought that was the purpose, for me to talk. He didn't want to deal with any issues. We took walks around the shopping center where his office was. We were talking about tennis one time, and he said, "Why don't we play sometime?" I didn't realize it then, but he was charging me for the time we played tennis.

I had two therapists after I came back to town, one a psychologist and one a psychiatrist, both of whom fostered my dependence on them. I believe a therapist should provide a client with tools so he or she doesn't need to keep coming back. Yes, I do have a lot of bitterness.

How long were you in therapy overall?

Two years as a child and a couple of years after I came back to town but was still attending college.

What finally led to your overcoming anorexia?

The second time I had anorexia, I was in the city living in an apartment close to the college. I got involved in theater and appeared in some plays. I found other outlets too—doing things with others and working at a bookstore, constructive pursuits which helped me refocus my energies. Because of the therapy, I was more aware of myself, more in touch with feelings, more able to detect when I needed to talk to somebody. One of the main problems that led to anorexia the first time was that I had always bottled feelings inside. The final breakthrough was learning to express myself, to articulate my feelings.

How do you feel talking about this now?

One of the things that bothers me is the stigma attached, the label "anorexic." In college I told one girl about it and afterwards she refused to be available when I wanted to talk.

You mentioned the difficulties in your relationships with your family. Can you describe them?

During my childhood, everything was really rigid and planned. We had piano lessons Thursday, other lessons Sunday, and, of course, school. Instead of going out to play, we would work with our dad on math problems—not schoolwork, just exercises he had us do.

The atmosphere at home was really strict, so there wasn't any real encouragement to socialize. My parents and my brothers were so close, I guess I felt ignored and wasn't sure if my parents loved me. I felt very intimidated by my father. He died during my junior year in college.

How do you feel now about your problems with anorexia?

To this day, the process of anorexia is frightening. Anorexics are pretty proud they can do what other people can't do—lose weight. On the other hand, bulimics are really ashamed of what seems to be their lack of control. Today I don't worry any more about my weight. I eat a balanced diet and don't concern myself with food.

Meg A.

Hospitalized when her menstrual periods stopped, Meg began to recover from anorexia when she realized how starvation was affecting her body. She knew she had to start eating in order to re-establish her menstrual cycle.

What was your life like when you first moved to Chicago?

When I first came to Chicago in October 1976, life was good. It got hectic as I tried to open a clothing store in 1977. The carpet I'd ordered didn't come in on time, and then a flood demolished the store in the fall of 1977. After these catastrophes, I began to evaluate my life and reassess what I wanted to do. I ended up opening another store in a suburb. But during the flood I met a man who was volunteering his time to pump out basements. We dated until January 1978, when he remarried his former wife. His remarrying really upset me.

When did your anorexia begin?

I began to lose weight when I went to a diet clinic in May 1978. I am five feet four inches tall and I weighed about 136 pounds. I was very serious about losing weight, but not obsessed with it. I think the anorexia began when I had lost enough weight so that people were beginning to notice. That felt good! I thought I'd just lose a little more, and that little became a little more, and so on.

Why did you decide to go on the diet?

I was almost twenty-nine years old. I decided that if I had to be twenty-nine, I didn't want to be twenty-nine and fat. Although I didn't blame my weight for the break-up with my boyfriend—I didn't even think about that—I became consumed with my weight while I was getting over his remarriage.

Lots of times now, however, I think the reason I'm not married and don't have a relationship with a man is because I'm overweight. I haven't dated anyone since this last experience; I think it takes at least two years to get over someone. I used to believe that if I were thin, a man would like me and take me away from all the chaos in my life. But that theory didn't work because I got too thin; men don't like you too thin either. The funny thing is: I can't remember being in between. I lost weight and then I gained weight. I can't remember ever thinking that whatever I weighed was the "right" weight. I never felt I was "there."

When did dieting get out of control?

During the fall of 1978 when I started working two jobs. I was an evening hostess at a restaurant and manager of a clothing store during the day.

What were your thoughts about food at this time?

I remember when the restaurant staff asked what size uniform I took, I answered, "A size eight." But actually I needed the smallest one they had—a size four. I thought that was *wonderful!* All I ever ate were fruit and salads at the restaurant. Even though they had other marvelous foods, I never ate any of them.

Were you aware of being hungry?

I don't think I was ever very hungry. I felt so good being in control of the situation, even though there were times when I would pass out. I went through a period of having diarrhea and all sorts of other disorders. But that was at the beginning of the diet, probably because my body was not used to dieting.

I really had no idea there was anything wrong with me. I had never heard of anorexia, and no one ever suggested to me that I might have it. In November or December of 1978 I lost a lot of weight really fast. I quit having periods in October at 110 pounds. In January, when I went to see my family doctor, I weighed 87 pounds, but he didn't suggest there was anything wrong with me.

You said you were proud of your control during that time . . .

Oh, yes, I was! I remember one time going out with two friends to a Mexican restaurant and eating hardly anything—just a little thing with lettuce on it, not even a taco salad. I was in total control of my food intake, you know. This was something I really could control. Other things—the flood, the break-up, the closing of the first store—I couldn't control, even though it took me a long time to convince myself that I didn't *cause* the flood or *cause* the store to close.

And during all this time no medical professional thought it was odd that your weight was so low?

I called a gynecologist in October of 1978 and told her that my periods had stopped and that I had lost a lot of weight. She said, "Don't worry. They'll come back." Actually, I thought it was wonderful not having periods. I wasn't very concerned about it. Then I started having really terrible water retention. A friend who worked for me forced me to go to a doctor, so I went back to the family doctor I mentioned earlier. He gave me birth control pills and a shot. My periods did not start again, but I felt I'd done what I could about it and I didn't worry about it.

When I went back to the gynecologist for my yearly checkup in April 1979, she said, "Why didn't you tell me you were so thin?" And I said, "I tried to tell you when I called you in October." She gave me estrogen and Provera for two months to start my periods. By August, nothing had changed, so she said, "I can't do anything more," and sent me to another doctor.

And still no one questioned why you were losing weight?

No. I will never forget calling the next gynecologist for an appointment. When I asked the nurse what kind of a doctor Dr. M. was, she said she specialized in infertility. Infertility! I never dreamed my problem was that severe. Dr. M. put me in the hospital for four days in October of 1979 to find out if I had diabetes and God knows what else! I was also seeing a dermatologist for an acne problem that had become really bad again after I went on the diet. The dermatologist told me I had Addison's disease. I went flying out to the library to find out what Addison's disease is. [Addison's disease is an adrenal gland insufficiency.—Ed.]

When did you begin to realize what was wrong with you?

Sometime during my hospitalization I became aware that *I* was causing my thinness by not eating. I had recently learned a little about the disease of anorexia and I asked the gynecologist if I had it. She told me I probably did, but that she wasn't going to write that in my diagnosis because, she said, "You don't want to have that hanging over your head."

I received no indication that I needed psychotherapy. The gynecologist sent me to an endocrinologist, who in turn sent me to a dietitian. This "pass the patient" game was their way of helping me.

In the spring of 1980 the dietitian gave me the book *The Golden Cage* by Hilde Bruch. As I read it, I decided that I must have had anorexia. I remembered having experiences like those of the anorexics described in the book.

I was on my feet all day at the store and then again until 1:00 A.M. at the restaurant. If I had eaten two extra oranges from the amount I'd allotted myself, I would walk up the back stairs, down the front stairs, and back up the back stairs over and over again to make sure I burned up those calories. I seemed to have extra strength—I didn't feel sickly. I must have had a lot of time on my hands then, because I remember walking all over the city for hours on Sundays.

When did you start to gain weight from your low of 87 pounds?

After I was in the hospital, I decided that something was wrong with me and I wasn't eating enough. Earlier both doctors had suggested I eat more, but at the time I just didn't pay any attention to them because I didn't want to do it. The endocrinologist encouraged me to eat red meat, which really made me sick. It was too rich and gave me diarrhea.

Did you feel that your doctors were caring?

I think so. One reason I thought the second gynecologist cared about me was that she went to bat for me with the insurance company because my claim was turned down.

My mind was confused. I *liked* having something wrong with me, maybe for the attention.

Can you describe what has gone on in your life
from your hospitalization to the present time?

I probably weighed about 100 pounds when I first went to see the dietitian. It was when I started seeing the dietitian and housesitting that I started overeating and bingeing. I think it was because I was so miserable about having to housesit to make extra money.

These people had all this food in their houses—food I had never tasted before. At the beginning I would always binge at night and eat very little the next day. Then I'd do it all over again. I thought many times that I would go throw up after bingeing, but I never did because I would rather not eat than make myself throw up. With all this bingeing, my weight went up to about 140 pounds.

In the fall of 1980 I joined a behavior modification group for weight control. That didn't help my problem because I focused even more on food; it became even more of an obsession.

What helped you finally get over your obsession with food?

A woman I worked with at the store had helped build my confidence by telling me I was capable of having a better job. Just having the confidence to go after a new job—and changing my routine after getting the job—seemed to help me "get over" food. Also I saw a counselor for a few months who helped me feel better about myself because we centered on other things besides food. The food obsession seemed to be just the way my other problems came out.

What was your relationship like with your parents
when you were going through this?

I never even told them I was in the hospital. When I went home in June of 1978, after beginning the dieting in May, I passed out in the grocery store while shopping with my mother. She was somewhat concerned, but simply took me home, fed me lunch, and that was the end of it. My parents never said a word about my passing out, and I didn't see them again until the fall.

By then I was pretty thin. But they never commented that I was too thin, or that maybe I should gain some weight. My sister was concerned though.

What is your relationship with your parents now?

I get a letter about once a week from my mother. She makes me feel guilty because she says my sister is hard to talk to; she tells me she's lucky to have me. Then I think, "Gee, the things I say about *her!*"

When my mother calls, I try to be really nice to her. I feel as though I'm the one who is under pressure—from her. If she were a little different, I think I could feel more affection for her. It's not that I don't want to, but we just don't connect. My dad is kind of out in left field. I don't know what he's up to.

You know, it seems as though they were never really interested in what my brothers and sister and I were doing when we were growing up. They might have been, but I never thought they were.

I never gave them the opportunity to be disappointed in me. My sister, who's the oldest (I'm the second oldest), did well in school so I always had to measure up to her. If she was editor of the yearbook, I felt I had to be editor of the yearbook too.

My parents never had to reprimand me the way they did my two brothers. They were kind of worthless when they were young, but they turned out really well. I was always just really good.

I remember one time when my parents bought a new car, and I didn't like it. I heard my dad say to my mother, "Oh, don't worry about Meg. She'll be over it in a day." That's how they think about me. They think I get over things so quickly, but what they don't realize is: I don't. Most people usually can't tell when I'm in a bad mood.

Do you feel you would have fit the "perfect little girl" image often associated with anorexics?

Oh, yes!

What other feelings do you have about your experience?

I've always had a weight problem, so I'm not surprised that I developed anorexia. I think all the crises that were out of my control were probably the final straw. Before I read about Karen Carpenter and Cherry Boone O'Neill, I had no idea they were anorexic. After Karen Carpenter died, it really hit me how lucky I was not to end up like her. But I probably wouldn't have listened if you'd told me that then.

Around the time that I was in the hospital, I stopped starving myself. I thought: I don't want to go through this again, them poking me and doing all those tests and everything.

I think it was really sad that nobody tried to help me. Most of my friends were not concerned, except for one person who kept urging me to eat—but that only made me eat less. I wasn't particularly close to anyone. Years later, one friend said, "I was so concerned about you." But at the time almost no one seemed to be worried about my weight loss.

My parents never worried about me either. On the other hand, I think it can work against an anorexic if parents are *too* concerned.

As for the professionals—I would have thought that from the very beginning, starting with the first gynecologist, someone might have suggested that I needed help.

To give them credit, though, I doubt that I ever confessed that I wasn't eating much. And when I went to the gynecologist, I wasn't connecting my problems with what I ate; I thought I had some dread disease that made me lose weight. She seemed to think I had "exhausted adrenal glands."

I now think of anorexia as more of a mental than a physical disease. I never really asked for psychiatric help either, except when I went to a mental health agency. I didn't find that very helpful.

What was your experience at the mental health agency?

Once on my day off, I was feeling "undone" about everything. I walked into a mental health center and they assigned me to a woman. I talked with her for a long time, then went back for about nine more visits. I didn't dislike this therapist, but I didn't feel close to her either. We used to role-play what I was going to say to my mother on the telephone. That's what we talked about—my relationship with my mother. We also discussed the man I'd been dating who had remarried his wife.

Then one day I decided I'd had enough counseling. That was just before I went on the diet, in the spring of 1978.

I figured that, since the counseling hadn't worked, going on a diet and getting thin would solve all my problems.

What progress do you feel you've made since that time?

Well, I have feelings now. I wasn't aware of any feelings then. All my energies were consumed with my food obsession. I asked a friend who used to work for me if she ever noticed if I was in a bad mood, and she said, "No, except when you were so thin, and then you were really cranky."

Now I have all sorts of mood swings. I can cry at the drop of a hat. I didn't cry for at least two years when I was dieting.

I find that I need to slow down and enjoy what I'm doing *now* instead of always being in such a hurry or planning ahead all the time.

How has your attitude about weight changed?

After I went on my diet, I remember that I lost ten pounds and thought, "This is great! Let's lose another ten!" I weighed every morning. Then I became obsessed with the goal of weighing 100 pounds, so I watched every day for the scale to say 100. I got into a routine of eating certain little things. When I hit 100, it seemed easier to lose the last pounds. I used to go to the shopping center on my way to work and walk and walk.

When I gave up the diet and the exercise routine, obviously I gained weight. Now I am losing again, but gradually—my weight has dropped from 155 pounds to 140. I have stopped obsessing over my weight and food. Now I think it is perfectly fine to be just normal and healthy.

Joe F.

*After having lost ninety pounds, Joe F., a twenty-three-year-old
male, attributes his recovery partially to the people who worked
with him during his latest hospitalization. The process of recovery
began with the relationships he formed in the hospital, with the
renewal of his relationship with his father, and with a special
friendship with a young woman. Taking responsibility for his own
recovery is also an important factor in helping him gain back his
health.*

How would you describe your childhood?

My parents were divorced when I was ten years old. At that time there
were five children in our family. I was pretty crushed about the divorce;
it hurt a lot. Then my mother was remarried—to a man who had nine
kids. At first this took some adjusting to, but then I grew to feel that my
stepbrothers and stepsisters were my actual family. There was a
closeness, even though no one in our family shows much emotion.
Because we didn't let our emotions show, when I would have a "big"
emotion, I hadn't learned what to do with it.

All of us were expected to achieve. Both my real father and my
stepfather are self-made men who are very wealthy and very successful—leaders in their fields with national recognition. I felt—and still
do—that I have a lot to live up to. Although they don't say so, you just
know they have high expectations.

As a matter of fact, *I* feel the need to succeed. I've always had a lot
[of material comforts] and have grown used to a certain standard of
living. This means that I'll have to succeed in some material way in
order to maintain that lifestyle.

Also, our family has always been very health-conscious. In high
school, I was a big athlete. I played football and was a die-hard skier.
Not only was I a ski instructor, but also a ski racer on a team.

Did you worry about your weight then?

No. I am five feet ten inches tall. I weighed 190 pounds during football season. I was pretty well muscled then and never considered myself fat, just pretty solid. When I wasn't playing football, I was training for or participating in the next sport. My usual weight was 175 pounds, except when I peaked out at 190 pounds for football.

How old were you when you first developed anorexia?

I was twenty years old and a student at an art school when my relationship with a girlfriend ended. I was devastated. I became severely depressed and was suicidal during the year after this happened. The breakup happened in the spring and I was so immobilized that I couldn't go back to school the next fall.

In fact, it was during my hospital stay for this depression that I became acquainted with several girls who had anorexia. At some point, I *chose* anorexia—not consciously—as a way of dealing with my problems, rather than continuing to be depressed and suicidal.

I wasn't obsessed with food while I was growing up. I don't know why I didn't become an alcoholic or addicted to drugs. I really don't know why I happened to become anorexic.

I started eating less and less because I was so depressed. When I left the hospital, I stopped eating altogether and the obsession with food began. The more weight I lost, the more obsessed I became.

I was living with my mother and stepfather and brothers and sisters and would do the meal planning and preparation to help my mom. I was completely preoccupied with food. In looking back, it seems to me I was a typical, textbook anorexic.

What prompted you to seek help for your anorexia?

By this time, I had lost most of my friends because during those months I was so depressed, I had withdrawn from most of them; I was totally alienated. Besides, many of them were friends my former girlfriend and I had shared. I couldn't risk running into her.

I continued in therapy during the period following my hospitalization for depression. The therapist and my parents would tell me I was losing too much weight; finally, they decided I had lost so much that I was reaching the danger point. My weight got down to 100 pounds. Also, I had begun to binge and purge during this time of starvation. I felt that the bingeing and purging had to stop. I was scared to death that I would gain weight from the binges, even though I didn't.

I didn't see myself as too fat; I wanted to lose weight to be more in shape. It was a real obsession—to lose weight and exercise. Any extra moment I had I would be doing something physical. I wasn't too worried over the starving, but the bingeing and purging were really getting me down. In fact, I really enjoyed the starving and really enjoyed losing weight. I agreed to go to the hospital because I hated the bingeing and purging.

It (the initial hospitalization and treatment) was a disaster! They immediately put me on hyperalimentation—feeding through the veins. I hated it! Even though the staff thought I was near death and that no psychological treatment was possible at the time, I felt it was the worst thing that happened to me—this forced feeding. When that happened, I was dead. They had taken my life—my power—away. It was degrading, humiliating, painful, frightening. I couldn't shower because of the tubes; it was terrible. When I got up to 125 pounds, they took away the intravenous feeding. Then I would hide my food and would drink huge quantities of water to weigh more. I would also tape quarters to my crotch in order to weigh more. The dietitian was trying to monitor my food intake. I probably knew more about calories than she did. After about eight weeks of this, the hospital staff confronted me with my behavior. They informed me that I could choose to go along with their treatment program, or I could leave the hospital AMA (against medical advice). I left AMA.

After I left the hospital, I continued my alternate starving and bingeing and purging. My mother and stepfather were fed up by now with my behavior and issued an ultimatum, that I could either eat normally and live at home or leave. I didn't feel I could make that promise, so I left.

What happened then?

I got an apartment of my own and went back to school, a different art school this time in my home state. I was doing exceptionally well at school. Being a supreme perfectionist, not only would I do the best job possible on my assignments, but I would do them far better than the instructors expected. I was the best—really good!

I was literally dying. I decided at this point that I did want to live. I dropped out of school then in the middle of the year. I planned to get a

job, solve my eating problems, and then go back to school. My real
father gave me a job as a clerk with his company. This kept me busy,
but I was still deteriorating physically.

Then I heard about this eating disorders unit in another state because
a friend of my mother had been there. I decided to go.

At first, I felt it was going to be another power struggle between me
and the hospital, but it didn't turn out to be that way at all. I almost left
after the first three days. Then they gave me the ultimatum that they
would "commit me," which meant I would have had to stay for at least
six months. I didn't want that to happen [commitment], so I chose to
stay voluntarily. I stayed for ten weeks and worked hard with the
program.

A big turning point in my recovery was this last hospitalization—the
people who work in the program and the way the program was
designed made it a really positive experience.

One phrase I learned in the hospital stands out in my mind as
having a major impact on my recovery—"I'm sick and tired of being
sick and tired."

This disease (anorexia) is really a killer. To recover from it, it seems
you really have to hit rock bottom. I began the process of getting well
when I took on the responsibility for my own recovery.

What has your life been like since your last hospitalization?

I came back to Minnesota and moved in with my dad, who was living
by himself. My relationship with my father has gotten a lot better than
it used to be, and this has been a tremendous help in my recovery. The
communication between me and my dad is very important to me—
between me and anyone, really.

I learned how to express my feelings during the hospitalization and
to communicate them to other people. So now I'm able to be more
open about things—I'm dealing up front with my problems, rather than
starving or purging. Even though my family members may not be
changing much in their ability to express their own feelings, I feel my
own change in this area has been another major factor in my recovery.
It still matters to me that they have problems expressing themselves,
but I am getting better at accepting that they're not able to be as
expressive as I'd like them to be.

Through my therapy in the hospital, I have learned that I am the
only person I can be responsible for; I can't be responsible for my

mom's feelings, or anyone else's for that matter. I also know that I am responsible for my own recovery. I can choose to die if I want to or I can choose to recover. And I realize I am not alone.

The four most instrumental things in my recovery are my family, my friends, my Higher Power, and myself. Friends include all the people I worked with in the hospital, the others with eating disorders, and a girl I consider my best friend.

I met her when I was hospitalized for depression and she was a student nurse there. During that hospitalization, she made me feel she cared for me as a person. I tried to be friends with her when I left the hospital, but she said she could not at that time, for professional reasons. Then one day she did call me up to wish me a happy birthday. Since then, we have become really good friends. As I said earlier, she is the person I consider my best friend. Although the friendship with her was not *the* single "turning point," I certainly value it as an asset to my recovery.

How do you feel talking about your experience with anorexia?

It doesn't bother me because I feel my story might be of some help to others with eating disorders, to give them hope for recovery. When I read Cherry Boone O'Neill's book, I really identified with her. Except for the fact that her father is Pat Boone, a famous singer and actor, I felt it was my story too. I saw all sorts of similarities between our family structure and hers, between her situation as she grew up and my own. Expectations and perfectionism have been issues in her life too.

How much do you weigh now?

Thinking about my weight tends to "send me off." The last time I weighed it was 120 pounds. My lowest weight was 100 pounds.

What other feelings about your experience would you like to share?

I feel frustrated all the time because I still want to keep my disease. I wish that I didn't have to eat. There is an internal struggle still going on. I still sometimes think about not eating. I am still working through this obsession. However, I am living again and do feel that I am on top of it right now. I am maintaining my recovery by being more open, more assertive, more aware, making my recovery my number one priority. I no longer expect myself to be perfect on my road to recovery or perfect in anything. That only sets me up to be one mistake from failure.

When I got around to thinking more "straight," some of the things I did seemed mind-boggling to me. For instance, it's very hard for me to believe the binges I used to have. At one time, two oranges would be a binge for me. Later, a typical binge would be two large pizzas, one cake, one dozen cookies, one dozen doughnuts, one box of cereal and a gallon of milk. It was nothing for me to spend sixty-five to seventy dollars for a binge. Then I would purge (vomit) and take large quantities of laxative tablets. They were a stimulant type of laxative—the most dangerous kind to abuse this way, I've been told.

I went through this ritual every night for close to a year. I would be wiped out physically until the next night and then would start all over again. I used to read all of the books I could find on eating disorders, not to learn how to get better, but to learn how to be a more perfect anorexic. Since I was released from the hospital about six months ago, I have only performed this ritual a handful of times and not at all for the past month. My recovery takes several steps forward and occasionally one step backward, but that's okay. I don't feel the need to be perfect in my recovery, either.

Altogether, I went through about $20,000—spending it on food and laxatives. I would never steal, though. I'm too honest for that. This was money that had been set aside for my college education. Even though the money was mine, I have almost dedicated myself to earning it back.

What are your plans for the future?

I have never completed my degree, but right now, I feel that going back to school would mean too much pressure. I don't want to set myself up for failure.

I am doing a good job working for my father now. I'm beginning to like learning about how his business works, which is a sentimental thing for me. We have a mutual ground for talking; it's a starting point. The process of recovery is slow, but it's happening. I didn't have my real father around when I was little, and it's too late for that. But we can be good friends now.

Part Two

Anorexia nervosa: What it is and what can be done about it

The following chapters give background information about anorexia nervosa from the points of view of two physicians (a psychiatrist and an endocrinologist) and the two authors (one a registered dietitian/nutrition counselor and the other a journalist specializing in health and family life, who is also a concerned parent).

The authors' commentary points up parallels in the anorexics' stories, offers a perspective on male anorexia, and summarizes the probable relationship between our society's overemphasis on a trim-and-fit body ideal and the growing problem of eating disorders.

A psychiatrist's overview of anorexia nervosa

Frederick Stuart Mittleman, M.D.

In the treatment of anorexics, bulimics, and their families in my psychiatric practice, I am particularly aware of the need for first-person information from those who have suffered with eating disorders, as well as from the professionals who have treated them.

The purpose of this overview is to offer information about anorexia nervosa—what it is, possible causes, how it is diagnosed, incidence, mortality rate, and treatment. It also gives a psychological and sociological profile of the typical anorexic, as well as some psychological warning signs to help families and others identify anorexics.

What is anorexia nervosa?

The simplest definition of anorexia nervosa is "a condition of self-starvation." The label "anorexia nervosa," assigned to self-starvation more than 100 years ago, really is an inaccurate name for the illness. Anorexia means lack of appetite, yet those who suffer with anorexia are obsessed with thoughts of food and its preparation while they deny their own hunger and need for food.

What causes it?

The condition of self-starvation was described at least as early as 1694 and has long been the subject of medical investigation. Research continues on anorexia nervosa, as theories about its cause and development are being explored, discussed, and supported by an accumulating body of evidence. A major issue, far from being resolved, is whether the origins of anorexia nervosa are psychological or physical.

As a possible physical cause, Vigersky (1976, 1977) raises the possibility that anorexia nervosa may begin with a disorder of the hypothalamus, a gland that produces hormones which regulate many of the body's functions. Among these functions are thirst and water metabolism; hunger and satiety; temperature regulation; and endocrine gland regulation (these glands include the thyroid, adrenal, testes and ovaries, and pituitary).

Hilde Bruch (1973) supports the theory of psychological origins. She believes that the symptoms of anorexia (self-starvation and weight loss) are late developments in the course of the disease, the main issues being "a struggle for control, for a sense of identity, competence, and effectiveness."

Bruch has identified areas of disturbed psychological functioning in the typical anorexic: a disturbance in body image and concept (anorexics typically view themselves as fat, even when they are emaciated); the inability to recognize and interpret accurately body signals such as hunger, fatigue, reaction to external changes in temperature, sexual feelings, or emotions; and a crippling feeling of ineffectiveness, of helplessness, which affects all thinking and doing.

Other proposed causes of anorexia include societal pressures to be thin, changing roles and interactions within the family, increased pressures on women. Also cited are the anorexic's avoidance of post-puberty conflicts, fear of oral impregnation, and psychiatric disturbances such as depression.

With the incidence of anorexia nervosa increasing, some credibility can be given to the thin-is-in pressures of today's society—the looming fear of being fat which seems to affect people of all ages.

Also, family interactions are shifting, especially with more mothers working outside the home. A woman now expects to achieve success in a career, be physically fit and attractive, have a good relationship with a spouse or other important person in her life, and be a caring, effective parent. Many women expect to be perfect in all these areas—the superwoman syndrome. When reality does not meet their high expectations of themselves, they feel guilty and inadequate. Young girls early become aware of the multiple areas they are now expected to excel in, and mature women sometimes feel like perpetual failures because they cannot meet their own—and frequently others'—expectations. The unemployed mother or wife today may feel guilty because she assumes she is a non-productive member of society. Therefore many women are caught in high-pressure, high-tension situations and have not learned positive ways of coping with them.

They look for an outlet for the tensions of having failed to meet expectations, as well as a reason for what they perceive as failures. Some focus on their appearance and believe "if only I were thin, things would be perfect." Dieting and obsession with losing weight may serve as an escape from other frustrations.

Obviously the issue of cause and effect of anorexia is not simple. My opinion is that there is a biological predisposition toward anorexia that is activated by psychosocial factors. In my view, societal pressures definitely contribute to the increased incidence of anorexia and the related disorder, bulimia.

It is possible that anorexia is not a single disorder but may take several different forms with different causes. The psychological and biological factors and their interactions that may be responsible for one form of anorexia may be different from those involved in another form. For example, one of the diagnostic criteria for anorexia—cessation of menstrual periods—has been found to begin *before* loss of weight in many anorexics. In others, menstrual periods cease only *after* a substantial amount of weight has been lost.

A psychological factor such as the stress of leaving home and going away to college, has been found to influence the hormones that regulate the menstrual cycle. Often I have observed a strong "separation anxiety" in my anorexic patients—a fear of separation when confronted with leaving familiar surroundings and situations. The person feels unable to cope with newness. The onset of anorexia is often associated with moving to a new residence or school—times when parents, friends, well-known places are left behind—or when other psychologically stressful life changes take place.

How is anorexia nervosa diagnosed?

Whatever the origin of anorexia, the criteria for diagnosis outlined by the American Psychiatric Association in its *Diagnostic and Statistical Manual of Mental Disorders (DSM III)* include the following. The person:

- Has an intense fear of becoming fat. This fear of fat does not decrease even when significant amounts of weight have been lost;

- Continues to "feel fat" even though emaciated;

- Has lost more than 25 percent of original body weight;

- Refuses to maintain a normal body weight for her/his age and height;

- Has no known physical illness that could account for the weight loss.

Although referred to by many as a disease, anorexia nervosa is more accurately called a "syndrome," a group of symptoms or signs that characterize an abnormal condition. As anorexia progresses, other signs may appear: thinning hair on the head; the appearance of downy body hair (lanugo); lowered body temperature; low blood pressure (80/50 is not uncommon); low pulse rate; complaints of feeling cold; dry, flaky skin, sometimes grayish in tone (with extreme weight loss); constipation; insomnia; hyperactivity. One of the most telling symptoms of anorexia in young women is that their menstrual periods stop (or with pre-adolescent girls, the periods never start).

How many teenage girls have anorexia?

The statistic I usually cite is that 1 in 100 teenage girls will struggle with anorexia. However, several studies provide information about some specific population groups. Nylander, in a 1971 study of a Swedish adolescent population discovered anorexia in about 1 in 150 teenage girls. Crisp, in a later study in England (1976), estimated that 1 in 200 teenage girls had anorexia in a severe form. In a 1983 study of English day-school students, Szmukler found the incidence of anorexia to be 1 in 120 girls; for those over age sixteen the incidence was 1 in 90. The researchers in Szmukler's study claim that many other girls showed a partial syndrome of anorexia nervosa.

How many die from it?

The death rate from anorexia nervosa appears to be in the range of 15 to 21 percent *(DSM III, 1980)*. Suicide, malnutrition, infection, and sudden death as a result of electrolyte disturbances are among the causes. (Elecrolytes are chemicals surrounding cell membranes inside and outside which are major forces in controlling fluid balance in the body. An electrolyte imbalance may lead to arrythmia—an irregular heartbeat—that can be fatal.)

What is bulimia?

Bulimia is an eating disorder which is related to anorexia and defined as "binge eating" or "insatiable appetite" with or without self-induced vomiting. Only as recently as 1980 was bulimia listed by the American Psychiatric Association as a psychiatric disorder. To quote the *DSM III*:

"The essential features (of bulimia) are episodic binge eating (rapid consumption of a large amount of food usually in less than two hours) accompanied by an awareness that the eating pattern is abnormal, fear of not being able to stop eating voluntarily, and depressed mood and self-deprecating thoughts following the eating binges."

A 1981 study (Halmi et al.) showed that as many as 19 percent of college women who responded to a survey met the *DSM III* criteria for bulimia. This is a truly frightening epidemic! However, in my experience I have found that most bulimics are not anorexic and a minority of anorexics are bulimic. I believe that, in most cases, bulimia is an illness separate from anorexia.

An often-quoted statistic is that approximately 25 percent of anorexics succumb to food binges. Binges may be followed by use of an enema, laxatives, diuretics, or by self-induced vomiting in an effort to rid the body of the food. Halmi and Falk, in a comparison of the characteristics of anorexics who exclusively starve themselves (exclusive or restrictive dieters) with anorexics who binge eat and then vomit (bulimics), found that the exclusive dieters were more depressed than the bulimics before treatment and at one-year-follow-up assessment. Bulimics were "a more chaotic group with personality disorder features of lying, 'psychotic tendencies,' and stressed interpersonal relationships."

My experience tends to support the findings of Halmi and Falk. I find that anorexics are unable to realize they have a problem. Bulimics realize their behavior is abnormal, feel ashamed, and try to hide the behavior. Because they are more secretive and often do not show a severe weight loss, bulimics can be more difficult to diagnose than anorexics, who are visibly underweight.

Recently some who treat bulimics have noted a relationship between bulimia and abuse of alcohol or other drugs. Dorothy Hatsukami and

her colleagues at the University of Minnesota medical school reported
that of 108 bulimics treated at the school's eating disorders program
over two years, 18.5 percent had a diagnosis of alcohol or drug abuse.
In Atlanta's Decatur hospital, 40 percent of the women treated for
bulimia "also have problems with alcohol and drugs," according to
Judith Knith, director of a Decatur program that treats eating disorders
as well as alcohol/drug problems.

What kind of person has anorexia?

Typically, anorexia has been associated with white twelve-to-eighteen-
year-old females from middle and upper middle socioeconomic levels. A
widely publicized diagnostic criterion (Feighner et al, 1972) was that the
age of onset of anorexia was below twenty-five.

Now, although the usual age still is in the range of twelve to thirty,
more and more women in their thirties, forties, fifties, and even sixties
are found to have anorexia. A recent case of a seventy-five-year-old
woman anorexic has come to my attention. Among those who develop
anorexia, the most frequently seen estimate is that 90 to 95 percent are
female, 5 to 10 percent are male. However, some recent figures show
the percentage of male anorexics as high as 15 percent.

What are the psychological symptoms?

An anorexic may show various psychological signs: body dissatisfaction
(feeling too fat), pursuit of thinness, hyperactivity (excessive physical
activity), food restriction, binge eating and/or vomiting (bulimic symptoms), use of diuretics or laxatives, low self-esteem, perfectionistic
qualities (wanting to be perfect, the best), compulsive behaviors
(especially having to do with food and diet), fear of change, and feelings
of sadness.

What about the families of anorexics?

I find that parents of anorexics are often resistant to change themselves.
Often they don't trust outsiders and believe they should be able to
handle all problems within the family circle.

There often is role reversal in these families; the child assumes a
parent's role and the parent assumes a child's role. For example, an
anorexic child is often responsible for the care of an ill or otherwise

impaired parent or takes on the responsibility of the household to "help" or protect the parent.

Typically, these families have problems expressing negative emotions, such as anger or hurt or disappointment. Often the person in whom anorexia develops is seen as never causing any trouble; she is the "good little girl." All children have negative emotions and these emotions need to surface in some way. For some "good" children, development of anorexia is a pathological outlet for emotions they find difficult to acknowledge or express—anger, resentment, or sexual feelings.

What are the warning signals?

When these "good" children characteristically do not express negative emotions, parents should be aware that this is not a normal pattern of behavior and may be a warning sign of a serious personality disturbance.

Other warning signals parents and others should watch for in children or teenagers are preoccupation with their bodies; unusual changes in behavior patterns with relation to food; and preoccupation with weight loss. Other signs are secretiveness, including the desire to be alone while eating; withdrawal from friends (increasing isolation); frantic physical activity; threats of self-destruction. Any of these signals should be taken seriously.

How is anorexia treated?

As stated earlier, the cause of anorexia is uncertain; the disorder may have a biological, psychological, or sociological origin. Most likely it involves an interplay of all three.

Methods of treatment are no less sure; a variety of approaches continue to be tried (Rockwell et al, 1982). These include forced feedings (tube or intravenous); forced fluids; psychoanalysis; psychotherapy with the individual and/or family; behavior therapy; hypnosis; neglect (no treatment at all); administration of medications such as thyroid extracts, steroid hormones, female hormones (estrogens, progesterones), pituitary extracts, L-dopa (used in the treatment of Parkinson's disease and not successful to date in the treatment of anorexia), chlorpromazine (used in the treatment of schizophrenia and known to produce weight gain in patients with this condition), cyproheptadene (trade name Periactin, used in the treatment of asthmatics and found to produce weight gain), and amitriptyline (an antidepressant that has also produced weight gain and a craving for carbohydrates). None of these drug therapies has been totally satisfactory.

Some of the behavior patterns of anorexics can be attributed to the fact that they are starving. Preoccupation with food and eating has been observed in other instances of starvation (Keys et al, 1950). Anorexics differ from other starving people, though, in their denial of the need to eat. The first goal of treatment is the restoration of adequate nutrition. Dietary treatment is combined with or followed by the use of some form of psychotherapy.

I believe that hospitalization is needed if 25 percent of the ideal body weight has been lost. If the female patient weighs only 80 to 85 pounds, she is definitely at risk. Whenever possible, it is desirable for the anorexic to decide to admit herself to treatment. I cannot say, "Come on in and let us take care of you." The situation may require that I be prepared to say, "Come back and see me when you are ready to begin treatment," even when I fear for the individual's safety. In my opinion, treatment is not successful unless the decision is the individual's. This gives the anorexic some control—something she or he badly needs. The anorexic makes the choice.

It is important for the individual's family to understand the need for treatment so they can help confront the anorexic's denial and encourage treatment. The encouragement should be based on the individual's behavior and her/his medical condition—and accompanied by firm resolve.

After the patient decides to go into treatment (in a hospital or as an outpatient), a realistic food program needs to be planned carefully with the help of a dietitian. Without the restoration of adequate nutrition, effective psychotherapy is often impossible.

The usual hospital treatment team includes a physician, nurses, a dietitian, psychological counselors, and an occupational therapist. The multidimensional treatment plan, integrated and individualized for the patient, needs to be written and each point clarified with the patient and members of the treatment team. Since the patient lacks objectivity about her or his condition, it is up to the treatment team to set up a reasonable plan; it does no good to just tell the patient to gain weight. Team conferences are necessary throughout the treatment program.

The plan must include an expectation of what the anorexic should eat (no compromises allowed) and how much weight will be gained per day. About one-half pound per day is a reasonable expectation. The anorexic should be weighed daily, without clothes (usually in a hospital gown), but should not be told the weight. The patient knows, however, that if the weight goal is not met, a liquid dietary supplement will be added. Food intake is not negotiable. All eating is done with a nurse present, and the patient is monitored for at least one hour after eating. If not, she or he may vomit, exercise violently, or find some other way of getting rid of the consumed calories.

If this process does not result in a weight gain, the next step is to try tube feeding. If this gets no results, the last resort is hyperalimentation (feeding complete nutrition through the vein). In the hospital I have been associated with (Menorah Medical Center in Kansas City, Missouri), as in most others, hyperalimentation is rarely used.

Education is important; the patient must be educated about the disease and its effects, as well as about the goals of treatment.

Also, the causes of the patient's behavior must be explored through psychotherapy. Issues of powerlessness and control, dependence and independence, self-dislike and self-esteem are frequently on the treatment agenda.

Each patient has someone to talk to, someone who accepts her/him unconditionally, someone with whom she or he can form a close relationship. An important key to recovery from anorexia seems to be this building of an alliance, often a relationship with a qualified therapist. I feel strongly about the need for "quality" therapy. A therapist can be quite competent, but without a good understanding of eating disorders, he or she can do more harm than good to a person suffering from the eating disorders of anorexia or bulimia or obesity.

Group therapy may be used, with caution. Anorexic behaviors can be "catching," so group therapy is highly structured. Family therapy and evaluation are crucial to the recovery process.

How can families help anorexics recover?

Families and others can help by realizing that anorexia is a chronic problem with no easy answers and many potential causes. An anorexic can best be helped if the family is open enough to allow close examination of family interactions—to find out if the family is contributing unknowingly to the development and continuation of the problem—and is also willing to participate in a therapeutic process.

Families need to be aware that the process of recovery may take weeks or months—there's no pill to take. It requires a great deal of patience and persistence on the part of all involved.

Parents need to guard against allowing preoccupation with the "patient" and her or his behavior to overwhelm them, so that the patient and the disorder become the sole focus of family life. Some families become so concerned with "saving their child" that this salvation becomes the sole purpose of their lives.

A certain amount of responsibility for overcoming the problem needs to be placed on the anorexic . Many anorexics tend to blame all their problems and their behavior on other people. Family members should let the anorexic know they are supportive and willing to be involved in treatment but can only assume responsibility for their own behavior.

Frederick Stuart Mittleman, M.D., is Clinical Associate Professor of Psychiatry at University of Missouri School of Medicine and Medical Director of Research Psychiatric Center, Kansas City, Missouri.

An endocrinologist talks about consequences of starvation

Barbara P. Lukert, M.D.

Since anorexia nervosa is a condition of self-starvation, its effects can only be understood by knowing the physical and psychological consequences of starvation.

The human body has an awe-inspiring ability to conserve itself, an evolutionary gift of survival from prehistoric days when food supplies were erratic at best, when large supplies of food were available only periodically and long periods of fasting occurred in between. In those days the ability to store calories was basic to survival, since the body called upon its stored calorie supply during these periods of fasting. The human body has retained this mechanism to the present day.

Food calories come from carbohydrate, protein, and fat. The body uses these calories to meet its immediate needs for energy, to replenish and expand the store of glycogen (starch) in the liver and muscles. Glycogen is used to help maintain a steady level of blood sugar. Protein calories are used to replace the protein broken down in the tissues since the last meal. Finally, surplus calories from any source are stored as fat.

When starvation begins, the body undergoes hormonal and metabolic changes that lead to selective mobilization of these stored calories for energy. Muscle and liver stores of glycogen contain less than 2,000 calories and supply energy for a very short time. If starvation lasts more than two days, fat stores are mobilized as a source of energy. At the same time, amino acids (constituents of protein) are directed into glucose (sugar) formation to be used as an energy source, instead of being directed into rebuilding protein. This causes loss of muscle mass.

The brain normally needs glucose as a source of energy, but when starvation is prolonged, it will utilize ketoacids (produced from fat tissue mobilization), thus minimizing muscle tissue breakdown.

During the first week of starvation, up to one pound of muscle may be lost each day, in addition to one-half pound of fat. Obese persons also lose ten to thirty pounds of fluid, while non-obese persons lose four to six pounds of fluid during this time.

After the first week or so of total starvation, weight loss falls to one-fourth pound of lean tissue daily and one-third to one-half pound of fat.

Psychological changes, a result of starvation's effect on brain functions, are emotional alterations such as mood fluctuations and depression. These are certainly characteristic of some anorexics. Changes in the regulatory functions of the hypothalamus result in decreased sex drive and diminished appetite. (Diminished appetite is not usually present unless the patient is quite ill from starvation. Instead, the anorexic typically denies a desire for food.) Sex hormones are affected; females cease to ovulate and males have decreased testicular function.

Other physiological changes are a decrease in basal metabolic rate and in thyroid hormone levels. Blood levels of uric acid are increased. Calcium is lost from bone.

Obviously the physical consequences of anorexia are severe, and, if self-starvation is prolonged, can lead to death.

An individualized treatment plan is developed with emphasis on educating the patient about her or his nutrient needs for growth, development, and tissue maintenance.

Helping the anorexic eat and regain weight is mandatory. But caution is urged by Huse and Lucas (1983), who recommend small quantities of food at first, enough to maintain the anorexic's present weight. The person is afraid of becoming fat, so this limited feeding meets psychological needs. The Huse and Lucas method is to determine basal calorie needs and then to recommend an increase of 250 to 300 calories over the basal needs or above the patient's current intake. Calories are increased usually in increments of 200 per week, but more slowly if the patient cannot adjust psychologically.

The patient is prepared for an initial rapid regain of water weight as glycogen stores and electrolytes are replenished. Electrolyte monitoring (measuring blood levels of chemicals such as sodium and potassium) is important during this refeeding stage.

Even after a satisfactory nutritional state has been achieved, metabolic processes may not return to normal for some time, and the patient should be made aware of this. For example, menstruation may not resume immediately even though weight has been regained.

Of course, simply treating the physical symptoms of anorexia, even while educating the anorexic about the effects of starvation, has seldom proved to be effective. The psychological issues also must be addressed.

Barbara P. Lukert, M.D., is Professor of Endocrinology and Metabolism at University of Kansas College of Health Sciences and Hospital, Kansas City, Kansas.

Relationships as life lines

My [Patricia Stein's] first treatment contact with an anorexic came at a time when I felt totally unprepared to handle the responsibility. Sally (the name has been changed to protect her anonymity) was referred to me by one of the clinic physicians so that I could determine how many calories she was consuming. Having made that determination, I was then to prescribe an appropriate weight-gain diet.

Sally was twenty-two years old, was five feet six inches tall and weighed seventy-three pounds. Of course, she did not consume the number of calories I prescribed for her. My advice went unheeded. Her food records, which she kept faithfully, resembled those of an extremely compliant dieter trying to lose weight. She added no fat to food as seasoning, and her snacks consisted of celery sticks and tomato juice. Sally controlled the food preparation herself.

After a short time of working with Sally, I knew I was out of my realm, and I attempted gently to refer her to a psychiatrist for treatment. She refused to go. She explained that before she had come to see me, she and her parents had accepted referral to a psychiatrist. Her comments about this experience: "he made me feel like a liar" and "he made my parents feel like criminals, and I couldn't put them through that." Now Sally would not consent to be seen by a psychologist or psychiatrist, even by an anorexia nervosa treatment specialist. I was stuck.

For a year Sally and I worked together while I consulted a psychiatrist about her treatment. Her weight during this time remained around seventy-five pounds, never varying by more than one or two pounds.

She lived at home, was unemployed, and was not looking for work because, she said, "my mother needs me to help her." She was frenetically active, a fact her mother disclosed to me.

During the course of the year's work with Sally, the psychiatrist advised me to drop the focus on food and explore other issues with her. So we talked about her feelings about herself and her family, her plans, her dreams for the future.

"I think I want to work on this by myself for a while," Sally said one day, and I didn't see her for about a year after that. At the time she stopped her regular visits, I was frantic with concern over her health and completely frustrated with a seeming lack of progress. I was literally afraid she might die but was powerless to do anything, since she refused all other kinds of treatment, including hospitalization.

One day Sally suddenly reappeared at my office, looking healthy. She thanked me for my help. She weighed 100 pounds at the time of this visit and at that weight she looked completely different from the frighteningly thin, apathetic person I had known. I was tremendously relieved, but perplexed about how I had really helped.

Now, several years later, I have come to believe that it was not so much specifically what was said or done during therapy but the establishment of an accepting, empathic relationship between Sally and me that helped her begin her recovery. Sally felt my genuine respect and concern for her as an individual of worth.

I believe that the psychological conditions that contribute to effective therapy—empathy, warmth, respect, concern, valuing and prizing, openness, honesty, genuineness, intimacy, self-disclosure, and confrontation—as specified by Patterson in his book, *Relationship Counseling and Psychotherapy*, are as important in the treatment of anorexia as they are in the treatment of any other problem requiring psychotherapeutic help. Sally's refusal to accept a second referral to a recognized therapy source evidences not only a denial of her disorder but her fear of giving up a relationship in which she felt trusting and comfortable.

In our interviews with recovering anorexics, the importance of relationships as lifelines was repeatedly emphasized—sometimes with a friend, sometimes with a therapist (or therapists), sometimes with a group who shared the same problem. It is my belief that the relationship we found may have been the catalyst for helping Sally recognize her own worth.

Dr. John A. Atchley, psychiatrist and president of the American Anorexia/Bulimia Association, Inc., in an article by Kim Brown in

Parents magazine ("When Dieting Goes Berserk," April 1985), said: "A good working relationship with the therapist is the most important thing of all."

One woman we interviewed summed up her feelings about the impact a positive relationship (with a friend) had on her recovery: "She was someone who would listen to me, someone I could talk to. Having her friendship was one of the things that helped me most . . . She didn't pass judgments, which really helped. She just listened and accepted me for myself."

Bruch (1979) stated that, "The task of psychotherapy in anorexia is to help a patient in her search for autonomy and self-directed identity by evoking an awareness of impulses, feelings, and needs that originate within her. Therapeutic focus must be on the patient's failure in self-expression, on the defective tools and concepts for organizing and expressing needs, and on the bewilderment in dealing with others. Therapy represents an attempt to repair the conceptual defects and distortions, the deep-seated sense of dissatisfaction and isolation, and the conviction of incompetence." Bruch goes on to emphasize the importance of helping the client recognize her (or his) own worth and substance.

Bruch's statements about the healing process were underscored by most of our interviewees. Almost all said they had feelings of incompetence, of being isolated, out of control, and unable to cope. As they began to recover, they regained self-confidence and self-esteem, began to participate in family and other relationships again and to identify and talk about their feelings.

Other parallels and differences

Besides the importance of relationships in their recoveries, the experiences of those we interviewed illustrate other parallels.

With the exception of Christie, who twice developed anorexia, once at age nine and again at eighteen, almost all were in their twenties when they developed anorexia. They were at the upper edge of the classic age range of twelve to eighteen or above it.

Almost all in this group mentioned either overprotective or rigid—sometimes domineering—parents or disturbed family relationships. Two, Erin and Heather, seemed positive about their early years, but both had overprotective, though caring, parents. Several mentioned trying to live up to the high expectations of parents or family members.

Sarah, who suffered from anorexia for the longest time—twelve years—had an alcoholic mother. Sarah initially was diagnosed as suicidal, suffering from depression. She believes, in looking back at that time in her life, that this was not an accurate diagnosis.

In almost all cases, the women went to medical doctors because of physical symptoms, particularly when their menstrual periods stopped. However, anorexia was seldom mentioned by these physicians. One patient was subjected to exploratory surgery; several were given female hormone preparations to stimulate menstruation; one was told she was in premature menopause and would never bear children. (Of course, a few years ago doctors generally were not as aware of the syndrome of anorexia nervosa as they are today.)

Experience with a therapist was not always credited with a part in the recovery process. Since the word "therapy" encompasses a great variety of treatments, any overly simple conclusions may be inaccurate. But among the female interviewees for this book, Sarah, who had the most therapy, also was sick the longest. Meg, who reportedly had the least psychotherapy (initially none), overcame her anorexia and food obsession in the shortest period, approximately two years.

Christie felt downright bitterness toward several of her therapists. Heather did not realize she was seeing a doctor (who, she later learned, was a psychiatrist) for other than physical problems. Erin was the most positive in attributing her recovery to the help of a therapist. Laura received therapy only briefly and credited it with getting her involved in outside interests, although it was several more years before she considered herself recovered. Her major therapeutic relationship was with a friend who accepted her unconditionally.

Since many therapeutic strategies, from behavior modification and psychoanalysis to drug therapy, have been tried in the treatment of anorexia without consistent success, the unpredictability of a therapist's impact is not surprising. In a review article on the treatment of anorexia (Rockwell et al, 1982), the authors point out the difficulty of treating a disease when its cause is not yet known. The debate continues about the origins and treatment of this still puzzling syndrome.

Several of the women interviewed for this book voiced a plea that therapists be sure they understand anorexia and bulimia before attempting to treat these disorders. One said, "If he had known more about anorexia then, he would have been of more help." Another said, "Today I know that this was the wrong approach—to focus on the food— but my therapist, I feel, did the best he knew how to do at that time."

In fairness to the eating disorders programs now increasingly available in many parts of the country, we must point out that most of the women interviewed here had to deal with their problems before such programs were readily accessible. Only Joe, who most recently developed anorexia, began his recovery in an eating disorders unit which treats the "whole person," physically, mentally, and emotionally. Joe does credit the people he worked with in treatment—professionals and fellow patients—with helping him begin his return to health.

Behavior patterns and psychological signs

Each of the persons interviewed showed several typical psychological signs and behavior patterns associated with anorexia nervosa, such as body dissatisfaction, pursuit of thinness, excessive physical activity, food

restriction and food obsession, binge eating (a symptom of bulimia), low
self-esteem, perfectionistic and compulsive behavior, fear of change,
feelings of sadness, and denial of appetite.

Their own words paint the emotional picture.

From Sarah: "As a child I saw myself as ugly and fat . . . I felt scared
and unsure of myself . . . I ate popcorn and went on uncontrollable
binges . . . I had a severe problem with my self-image, paired with
constant insomnia . . . I was obsessed with food, with cooking, with
cookbooks . . . I weighed 115 pounds and felt grotesque. I was very
depressed about this weight gain . . . My weight did not drop and I felt I
had to hide."

The initial unhappiness with Erin's weight and appearance was not
her own but her mother's; so was the overconcern with diet. From
Erin: ". . . My mom was a professional model, and she always had me
on a diet to lose weight in high school—'to look good' . . . My constant
comparing myself with my mother reflected my general lack of self-
esteem." Then, as her disease progressed, "I could see I was thin, all
right, but I liked what I saw . . . I'd exist on some fruit and cottage
cheese . . . I didn't think there was a thing wrong with me or the way I
ate . . . I needed to see if it was okay to be me instead of what I
perceived others wanted me to be."

Parental pressure about food left its mark on Laura as well. From
Laura's father we hear: "One of these days, you'll regret that piece of
cake. The boys won't want you when you're big and fat." Laura said,
"When I was twelve or thirteen, I began trying to diet because I
considered myself chunkier than a lot of kids." Later on: "I ate the same
thing every day for six weeks at a time (300 calories a day) . . . I had to
have my own food by myself so I could pick at it . . . I was so proud of
myself and on a 'high' because I had finally found something I could do
better than anyone else." She continued: "I thought I would break this
thing, but each time I changed my food rituals, I would binge, and then
I would be right back into starvation. Starvation was the only thing that
made me feel secure . . . I used enemas, diuretics, and laxatives, but
basically food restriction and exercising."

The theme of body dissatisfaction is heard again from Heather as she
describes her feelings during high school years. "My high school years
basically were happy, but my spirits sank to great depths of despair
when shorts and swimming-suit weather appeared . . . I was the only
one—or so it seemed to me—with a big, flabby tummy and thighs and
squishy upper arms." At this time, Heather weighed 110 pounds at five

feet seven inches tall! She talks about her obsession with weight and diet: "I alternately binged and starved until I became so hung up on food that what I ate would make or break my day."

With all of these recovering anorexics, an obsession with food and diet was manifested at a time of a major life change. For Sarah, it was leaving home for college and then getting married; for Erin, getting married and then pregnant; for Laura, moving to a new city; for Heather, graduating from college and facing the decision of what to do with the rest of her life; for Christie, going away to school; for Meg, moving to a new city, finding a new job, and experiencing a failed love affair; and for Joe, ending a relationship with a girlfriend.

Heather's remarks about her lowest point in her disorder show her fear and desperation: "The day I graduated from college, I suddenly admitted to myself that I had no idea what to do with my life, no real goal for what I wanted to be when I 'grew up.' I was confused and scared, but I didn't know how to help myself." She continues: "I was not aware I had a problem . . . I was unable to think rationally because of my starvation."

From Christie, a familiar theme often expressed by others with anorexia: "The anorexia was my way of taking some control over my life." At the age of nine, she "felt powerless in my position in the family." Also from Christie at age nine, an atypical comment: "I was already a thin kid and never viewed myself as having a weight problem." Yet, the second time she struggled with anorexia, weight became an issue between Christie and her mother, since Christie was beginning to gain. "My mom said, 'Well, we'll have to put you on a diet.' At first I was really rebellious that I had to do that. Then I put myself on a rigid diet and started to lose weight . . . And then my mom said, 'You don't want to get any thinner,' but I just kept going."

Denial of hunger is a repeated theme too. Meg demonstrates this most clearly: "I don't think I was ever very hungry. I felt good being in control of the situation, even though there were times when I would pass out . . . This was something I really could control. The other things—the flood, the breakup (of a relationship), the closing of the first store—I couldn't control."

Meg said about compulsive and excessive physical activity: "I was on my feet all day at the store and then again until 1:00 A.M. at the restaurant. If I had eaten two oranges that I thought were extra from my allotted amount, I would walk up the back stairs, down the front stairs, and back up the back stairs over and over to make sure I burned up those calories. It seemed I had extra strength."

The women expressed either their own concern—or the concern of another family member—over their weight. All described the miserable effects anorexia had on their lives. Each said (not necessarily during the formal interview) that looking back on herself during the time of her anorexia is like looking at someone else, a stranger. Most also felt that the compulsive behavior they demonstrated as anorexics had been rechanneled, but that they would always behave compulsively about something.

Anorexia nervosa in males

Very little has been written about anorexia in males, possibly because only an estimated 5 to 15 percent of anorexics are male, according to articles and books on the subject. Bruch (1973) in her book, *Eating Disorders*, has a chapter entitled "Anorexia Nervosa in the Male," in which she describes five cases of "atypical" and five cases of "typical" or "primary" anorexia. Cases of male "primary anorexics" possessed many of the same physical and psychological features of young women with a diagnosis of "primary anorexia."

According to Andersen (1985), anorexia nervosa is likely to be underdiagnosed in males because patients are embarrassed to tell anyone of their symptoms, or they assume the problem occurs only in adolescent females. Physicians, too, may be unaware of anorexia in the male. Others have pointed out that extreme thinness can be better hidden by men's clothing than by women's. Some note that one of the most telling symptoms—the cessation of menstrual periods—obviously is not present as a clue.

Most therapists we talked with who have worked with male anorexics are unwilling to generalize from the few cases they have seen. But many report either that the incidence of anorexia in males seems to be increasing, or that more males are asking for help than ever before.

Because of the scarcity of information about males and anorexia nervosa, when males do surface with the syndrome, they are able to find few materials which can help educate them about their disorder. As for treatment—when anorexia is diagnosed in a man, he may be reluctant or at best half-hearted about being treated in an eating

disorders program with a group of women for what is generally thought
to be a female problem.

In my [Patricia Stein's] practice as a dietitian, I have worked with a
few males who appeared to have characteristics in common with female
anorexics—fear of being too fat, preoccupation with the ideal of the
"perfect" body, overly strict dieting with subsequent uncontrollable
binges, and hyperactivity.

Other therapists reported that many similarities appear to exist
between male and female anorexics. Joe even remarked about his own
case's similarities to a female's, through his response to Cherry Boone
O'Neill's book, *Starving for Attention*. "I felt it was my story." he said.

According to Arnold E. Andersen in *Practical Comprehensive Treatment of Anorexia and Bulimia* (1985), the criteria for diagnosis and the
psychological-sociological picture in male and female anorexics are
similar. Most male anorexics' symptoms appear during adolescence. In
both males and females, there is an increased incidence of anorexia
nervosa in higher socioeconomic groups, and self-starvation may begin
with a diet. Fear of fatness and pursuit of thinness are characteristics of
male anorexics, as well as female. Disordered reproductive hormonal
activity is present in both sexes, including decreased levels of sex
hormones.

As with female anorexics, there appears to be no single explanation
for the cause of the disorder in males. Males have been under less
social pressure to be thin than females, although this appears to be
changing.

For years the female body has been displayed and judged against an
ideal of perfection—in beauty contests, in pin-up posters, in magazines,
film, and television. Now it seems that the male body is similarly on
display and similarly judged; we see a growing trend toward the
glamorization and objectification of the male body.

The current emphasis on the "ideal body"—male or female—as thin,
"fit," and "in shape" has provided a script for our times. It is possible
that the "being in shape" mandate may be magnified for males.
Certainly some of the male anorexics (as well as bulimics) are athletes,
for whom hyperactivity or overexercise is a symptom.

The unfortunate self-consciousness that can go along with the
perception of having a less-than-perfect body may now be spreading to
the male population as well as the female.

Joe's story has many parallels with stories of the women interviewed.
Like Meg, Joe told about breaking off an important relationship, which

"devastated" him: "I became severely depressed and was suicidal." Like Sarah, Joe was hospitalized for depression. As Laura had done, Joe spoke of lofty parental expectations: "All of us were expected to achieve . . . Although they don't say so, you just know they have high expectations." Like Meg, who went up and down stairs over and over again to burn up calories, and like Laura, who went to a fitness center seven days a week, Joe threw himself into physical activity: "Any extra moment I had I would be doing something physical."

Other characteristics echo those of the women anorexics:

Food obsession: "I . . . would do the meal planning and preparation to help my mom."

Perfectionism: "Being a supreme perfectionist, not only would I do the best job possible on my assignments (at art school), but I would do them far better than the instructors expected. I was the best—really good!"

Isolation and alienation: "I had lost most of my friends, because during those months I was so depressed I had withdrawn from them."

Inability to express feelings: ". . . no one in our family shows much emotion. Because we didn't let our emotions show, when I would have a "big" emotion, I hadn't learned what to do with it."

Like Christie, who seemed to *choose* anorexia to take some control over her life in a family in which she felt powerless, Joe said, "At some point, I *chose* anorexia—not consciously—as a way of dealing with my problems rather than continuing to be depressed and suicidal."

Joe was beyond adolescence when he experienced anorexia, but so were several of the young women interviewed.

Joe's bulimic symptoms—the out-of-control bingeing and purging—led him to seek help.

Relationships were a major factor in Joe's recovery—in the treatment facility and later with his father and with a girl who had been a student nurse at the time of his first hospitalization.

Anorexia and the myth
of the perfect body

Two questions have repeatedly surfaced during the preparation of this book: Why is the incidence of anorexia nervosa increasing, and why are most anorexics women?

In our opinion, social phenomena provide an answer to both of these questions. As a dietitian who has worked with clients in the area of weight control for seventeen years, and as a concerned parent and journalist active in improving communication between individuals, we have become increasingly aware of how many more women today than ever before are obsessed with their weight, dieting, and food. They are continually comparing their bodies with the super-thin, "perfect" physical ideal of our times.

These are women whose self-concept seems to be dictated by what the scale shows them each morning. Many of them binge uncontrollably. The binge usually is preceded by a brief bout with a new diet or even a day or two of starvation as penance for the previous binge. Weight and mood are on a continuous roller coaster.

Even health professionals have been influenced by the present-day ideal of thinness. Why didn't the physicians who treated the women we interviewed link anorexia with the patients' weight loss and cessation of menstruation? If they did make the connection, why didn't they mention the possibility of anorexia to the patients?

An article in *Psychosomatics* (Gross, 1982) emphasizes this apparently all too common problem. Gross cites an instance in which a twenty-two-year-old woman, five feet five inches tall and weighing 95 pounds, saw two gynecologists and an endocrinologist because her menstrual periods had stopped. She was put through several physical tests with negative results. The endocrinologist referred her to a psychiatrist for possible emotional tension related to the cessation of her menses. Anorexia was finally mentioned to the patient as a possibility by the psychiatrist, a possibility she herself had suspected.

Gross wrote: "The question arises of why several physicians accepted as attractive a woman five feet five inches tall weighing ninety-five pounds. Western culture tends to consider excessive thinness an ideal, and this has an unfortunate influence on teenage girls."

Not only on teenage girls, in our opinion, but on women of all ages.

Adult pressures on teens

Most of my [Patricia Stein's] clients are women, as are most anorexics. Some are teenagers, as are many anorexics. The examples which follow illustrate the pressures that adults—particularly parents—exert on female teens to be thin.

Debbie was referred to me by her pediatrician because she wanted to lose weight. She was sixteen years old, five feet five inches tall, and weighed 131½ pounds. Her high school drill team instructor had benched her because she was one and one-half pounds over the weight criterion for her height. The high school, it seems, had stiffened its weight requirements because someone had complained about "the cows" allowed to participate on the drill team. Debbie was desperate and ready to do anything—including fasting—to bring her weight down so she could be reinstated on the drill team. Fortunately for Debbie, her mother did not push her to take the weight off.

Why would a pediatrician send this teenage girl without an obvious weight problem for help in finding a "diet" to lose about ten pounds? Why would the high school allow weight to be a criterion for drill team participation? Why would a high school respond at all to an unkind remark about "cows"? We don't know the answers to these specific questions, but "society" must be contributing to our preoccupation with thinness. So often, as this case demonstrates, a certain weight is equated with acceptance and success.

Parental acceptance is crucial to building a child's healthy self-esteem. Instead of feeling accepted, fourteen-year-old Karen realized that she was the despair of her parents because she was heavy. Her mother brought her to me for assistance in losing weight. Karen told me that her mother wanted her to go on a 330-calorie-a-day formula diet, even though I had tried to convey to Karen and her mother the dangers and futility of putting Karen on a strict diet. The father, in a joint session with the mother and me, maintained that he "couldn't stand fat people."

Imagine a young person in a home environment in which acceptance as a person is contingent upon size! Parents of overweight teens have no idea of the impact their focus on weight and food will have on their offspring for years to come. Many of my adult overweight clients remember vividly and still feel the hurt and frustration of trying to lose weight to please their parents. The feelings of rebellion against these early pressures still interfere with their attempts to lose weight. In at least half the cases in this book, parental pressure to lose weight was mentioned as an early feature in the development of anorexia.

Another frustrated—and thin—mother wondered why her overweight daughter Donna was so different in personality from herself and her other daughter who was thin. The implication seemed to be that if only Donna were thin, she would be more like the mother, and therefore the mother could accept her more easily.

Donna's father offered to pay her $600 if she lost fifty pounds in two months (impossible for even the most dedicated dieter). Father made his approval and monetary payoff contingent on the attainment of an impossible goal. Donna was caught in a no-win situation. Imagine how she felt when she ultimately—and inevitably—failed to attain this parental goal.

In our opinion, the family and school pressures on these girls emphasize the plight of overweight teenagers today. Many teens must find it difficult to believe in their worth as individuals when their acceptance by family and peers is based on how they look and how heavy they are.

The ideal—Marilyn to Twiggy

Contrast these teens' situation with the teen experience in the early 1950s, when "going on a diet" or worrying about weighing too much was not a major societal concern. People who were "too thin" often felt less than self-assured. Anorexia nervosa was not a topic of conversation in those days.

On the contrary, the more popular young women were usually plump and curvaceous. In the 1950s and early '60s, a comparatively fat (by today's standards) Marilyn Monroe was promoted as having the ideal female body. Then along came Twiggy, an anorexic-appearing model, who became the media's feminine ideal. The growth of dieters' groups (like Weight Watchers, Diet Workshop, Diet Center, Overeaters Anonymous, Why Weight, Weight Loss Clinic, Weight Losers Institute, and Lean Line) came simultaneously with the recognition in the late 1960s and 1970s that eating disorders, including anorexia and bulimia, were becoming widespread problems.

One has only to open the morning newspaper, read a women's magazine, or watch television to become instantly aware of the thinness of advertising models and movie and television stars today, as well as of aggressively merchandised weight reduction programs and products. It is no secret that tremendous media pressure is placed on women of all ages to be slim and therefore, it is implied, more desirable.

Power and powerlessness

The 1960s saw, too, another movement grow in momentum—the women's liberation movement, toward equality, self-worth, dignity, strength, and power for women.

Is the coexistence of these two movements, the explosion of the diet industry and women's liberation, a chance happening, a pure coincidence? Probably not. Most clients of diet-regulating centers are women, as are most anorexics and bulimics. Anorexia is one means that a girl or woman has to achieve control or power. For some, anorexia may be the only way they can perceive to gain a sense of achievement or accomplishment. It is a way to stand out.

But the "power" of an anorexic is illusory, for eventual physical debilitation brings with it powerlessness and dependence. Focus on diet, food, and losing weight is commonplace among many women when they feel overwhelmed with responsibility, when other aspects of their lives feel out of control.

The quest for thinness is in direct opposition to the principles of liberation for women. It tends to rob the seeker of dignity and power, since a person on a prescribed diet turns responsibility for the choice of food over to someone else. "The Diet" becomes the focus of life, and the person is haunted by the continual specter of failure.

The irony of the diet business is that 75 to 95 percent of dieters regain all the weight they have lost, sometimes adding more (Bray, 1980). Most dieters are doomed to repeat the dieting process over and over, emerging each time with a dwindling sense of self-worth and dignity.

Kim Chernin, in her 1982 book, *The Obsession: Reflections on the Tyranny of Slenderness*, raised some interesting speculations about thinness and social pressure. She wonders if men are becoming threatened by the emerging power of women. She and others wonder if the trend toward more thin, young models and few adult, full-figured females as erotic ideals in ads and movies, is the male way of turning away from this female power.

According to Chernin, "In the era of women's liberation, which is also the era of fat farms and the body's emaciation, popular culture begins to produce movies in which photographers, grown men, become entranced with the Pretty Baby who lives in a whorehouse" (a reference to the film of the same name about a teenage prostitute). Chernin's points are given some support by the recent appearance of news articles reporting an increase in child pornography and the emergence of pedophile societies.

Susie Orbach in her two books, *Fat Is a Feminist Issue* (1978) and *Fat Is a Feminist Issue II* (1982), offers her perception of the food-and-weight dilemma facing women. She contends that because of the extreme pressures to be thin, adult women with no history of eating problems can find themselves caught up in the latest dieting craze, and that dieting turns "normal eaters" into people who are afraid of food.

People who diet do learn to ignore the body's hunger and satisfaction signals and, after a time, are unable to recognize physical hunger. Anyone who works with overweight people has heard the refrain, "I can't tell when I'm hungry anymore. I can't remember the last time I was physically hungry."

Orbach (1978) reminds us also of women's difficulty in expressing unpleasant emotions such as anger because of early training that "nice girls don't get angry." Many women (and men too) eat when they are angry because they cannot express their feelings, sometimes because they have been taught not to, but often because they feel their own needs for emotional expression are not as legitimate as others'.

Many are afraid they will not please others if they admit they have needs too. Women are brought up to be the nurturers in our society. To quote Orbach (1982): "The roots of compulsive eating in women stem from woman's position in society—she feeds everyone else, but her needs are personally illegitimate. Food, therefore, can become a way to

73

try to give to herself. Her fatness can become a way to express a protest at the definitions of her social role."

For the anorexic, as for others with eating disorders, food and starvation or bingeing are not the issue. The quest for thinness may begin the process of anorexia but apparently this is the symptom, not the real problem. Underlying issues have to do with lack of self-worth and feelings of powerlessness.

Choices and recovery

Realizing and admitting that one *does* have a choice about how one lives life is the first step to self-help in recovering from anorexia. Then, as treatment professional Denise Perkins, M.A., describes the recovery process, "as confidence builds and self-esteem improves, each woman can discover better ways of nurturing herself. She can shift her focus from looking outside of herself for validation and approval to looking inward instead. She can build a supportive network for herself and begin the process of discovering what she 'wants' instead of what others think she 'should' be."

As the stories of recovery in this book prove, one does not have to be doomed to self-hate and other uncomfortable feelings which accompany self-starvation, or to undesirable eating habits.

Listen to these anorexics who have overcome the problem talk about the changes in their lives:

"I've stopped obsessing over weight and food."

". . . now I'm able to be more open . . . I'm dealing up front with my problems."

"I'm trying very hard to help my child's self-concept be as strong as it can be by building a strong self-concept for myself too."

". . . I started feeling better about myself and seeing friends. The cumulative effect of the therapy I'd had over the years helped me to be more comfortable with myself . . . Things finally came together for me."

"Today I don't worry any more about my weight. I eat a balanced diet and don't concern myself with food."

"Now, being on my own, I can steer in the directions I want to go."

"I became more in touch with my feelings, individuating myself from my family."

"Very gradually I became aware of the people around me and began reaching out to them, developing support systems."

"I have learned that I am the only person I can be responsible for . . . I also know that I am responsible for my own recovery."

"I've met two of my goals—not weighing every day and enjoying life!"

Social phenomena—like the elusive ideal of the thin-and-perfect body—can change only over time with a general awareness of their harmful consequences.

In the meantime, individuals, through personal choices, can set about changing their own lives.

As this book illustrates, each person suffering from anorexia is starving from more than a loss of nutrition. In order to recover, anorexics must see themselves as worthy of emotional and physical nurturing.

The young women and the young man interviewed here all expressed, in their own ways, the hope that this book may help others share their similar plights. Through this sharing, they can learn to accept themselves—with whatever they perceive as their imperfections—and to reach out to others to discover the soul-nourishment that self-starvation, ironically, may be denying them.

Eating Behavior Awareness Test

Unremitting societal pressure to be thin appears to be turning "normal" eaters into people who diet over and over and frequently binge compulsively. These people may go on to develop anorexia nervosa (self-starvation) or bulimia (bingeing often followed by purging).

Readers may use the following questions to determine if they need to seek help for problems with eating. (Since denial of an eating disorder is common, friends or family members, employers or co-workers may answer these questions for an individual who may be anorexic, bulimic, or a compulsive overeater.) If you answer "yes" to any of the following statements, you may have an eating disorder ranging from mild to severe. You may seek help from a competent counselor, or at a clinic or hospital which has a specialized eating disorders program.

Yes   or   No

_____   _____   I regularly starve (or restrict calories drastically).

_____   _____   I starve (or restrict calories drastically) to make up for my eating binges.

_____   _____   I binge-eat uncontrollably.

_____   _____   I binge and then vomit afterwards.

_____ _____ I binge and then take enemas or laxatives to avoid getting fat.

_____ _____ I take diuretics to help keep my weight down.

_____ _____ I have developed eating rituals—eating the same thing every day, for instance.

_____ _____ I try to hide the way I eat—my eating rituals or eating binges—from others.

_____ _____ I feel guilty after eating anything not on my "allowed" diet.

_____ _____ I sometimes feel guilty when I eat anything at all.

_____ _____ I think constantly about food—about what and when I can eat next.

_____ _____ I am obsessed with the preparation and serving of food.

_____ _____ I believe my problems would be fewer if only I were thinner.

_____ _____ I would like myself better if only I were thinner.

_____ _____ Every day (or week) I plan to start a new diet.

_____ _____ I think I am fat even though others see me as normal or underweight.

_____ _____ My self-worth depends on whether I have gained or lost weight that day.

_____ _____ I feel that others look down on me because I am too fat.

_____ _____ I sometimes feel depressed about my eating—or non-eating—behavior.

_____ _____ I feel the need to control my life through controlling my food intake.

_____ _____ I am proud of my ability to control my food intake and weight.

_____ _____ I am ashamed of my out-of-control eating binges.

_____ _____ I exercise excessively; I've become "hyper" about physical activity.

Suggested prevention guidelines

It is not known if anorexia nervosa or related eating disorders actually can be prevented. However, here are some guidelines which may help family members, friends, teachers, coaches, counselors, and others avoid contributing to the problems of eating disorders.

• Provide an accepting environment. Don't tie your approval of an individual to her or his eating habits or weight. Avoid saying things like, "You'd be so attractive if only you were thin" or "You'd attract a much better-looking (more successful, more intelligent) type of man (woman) if only you were thin."

• Avoid bribing a child or teenager to lose weight. Don't nag someone with messages to "clean up your plate" or "quit eating junk food (fattening or 'bad' food)." This may be counterproductive; it could result in the person resisting your verbal nudges and doing just the opposite of what you desire.

• Encourage healthy eating habits by example and by providing nutritious foods. Teach nutrition basics at home and at school.

• Encourage healthy exercise habits. Positive exercise habits can promote a better self-image.

• Avoid commenting positively or negatively about other people's sizes or shapes. An adolescent or adult with a shaky self-image will usually believe you are directing the comments at her or him. For example, "Ugh, look at the size of those hips—that woman is as broad as a barn." If a person believes she is too fat, she will assume you feel the same way about her as well. Conversely, a positive statement about another's body may mean "Why can't you look like that?"

• Help a young person develop a good self-image, accept herself/ himself and be comfortable with her/his own identity. Be positive in your comments about appearance or other behaviors. Avoid making disparaging remarks like "That dress makes you look fat" or "You're wearing the same size now as your sister did when she was two years older."

• Be aware of traumas and crises in a young person's life. Be willing to spend time listening and talking about the person's problems and dilemmas. Be sensitive to the person during these times and avoid shrugging off the problem as inconsequential. It may appear small from an adult perspective, but loom large in a young person's life. Provide support and encouragement during these times.

• If the young person begins to talk about "going on a diet," find out what else is happening in her life at this time. The underlying problem may not be food or diet, but something else—often feelings of inadequacy or powerlessness, of not being accepted. Professional help may be necessary to help work through these issues, for the young person in question and perhaps for you, as well.

• Be tolerant of weights that may be higher than you think they should be. Perhaps you—as all of us—have been brainwashed by the media's presentation of too-thin-to-be-healthy models and actresses as role models. An individual may be genetically programmed to be somewhat larger than the image that films, TV, fashion magazines—and even some health professionals—are promoting as the ideal.

• If weight loss is called for, help the person find a nutrition and exercise program conducted by a professional or team of professionals knowledgeable about eating disorders. Some doctors, registered dietitians, exercise physiologists, psychologists, or other qualified health specialists have training and experience in weight loss and eating disorders. But just because a professional holds these qualifications does not guarantee this special knowledge. Be sure to ask questions before enrolling in any weight-loss program, for yourself or your children.

• Provide your children (students, clients) opportunities for and assistance in developing responsibility and accountability for their own actions. Point out areas in which they can—depending on their age—safely and appropriately take control of their lives.

• As a parent, take a look at your own "fear of fat." Try to avoid communicating this fear to your children.

• Avoid making food or eating an issue—investing it with out-of-proportion importance.

• Try to avoid perfectionistic expectations of a young person, an over-emphasis on achieving.

• Try to develop a young person's awareness of feelings—by acknowledging and talking about them, and by sharing your own.

Help for anorexia nervosa and other eating disorders

To find a qualified therapist: Ask your family physician or other health professional to give you the name of a therapist who is experienced in treating eating disorders.

To find an eating disorders program: Check your local or state mental health agency or your phone directory's yellow pages or call one of the national groups listed here for names of inpatient and outpatient programs in or near your area. Inpatient programs, because of the physical aspects of the disorder, usually will be hospital-based. Many facilities treat anorexia, bulimia, and compulsive overeating (often resulting in obesity) in the same program.

Programs are most often multidimensional. Simply treating the physical effects while attempting to change eating behavior—although essential to recovery—does not address the whole problem. Some programs have adapted the Twelve Steps of Alcoholics Anonymous (AA) as an element of treatment and aftercare.

Ask questions like these:

What other elements of treatment are included? Medication? Education about anorexia? Nutrition counseling? Individual psychotherapy? Goal-setting and contracts? Body image therapy? Family therapy? Group therapy?

If group therapy is used, is it structured and monitored? Do groups include just anorexics or other eating disorders patients too? Counselors have reported that anorexic behaviors may be catching—that in a group made up exclusively of anorexics, they may become competitive about losing weight.

In spite of this problem, many treatment professionals believe strongly in the validity of the group experience—to help the anorexic feel less isolated and learn to acknowledge and share painful feelings with an understanding peer group.

Are core issues explored, such as power and control, self-esteem, independence, parental or other expectations, perfectionism, stress management, interpersonal difficulties and relationships, adaptability to newness?

Is the program flexible enough to allow for individual needs?

How experienced are the staff members in treating eating disorders?

What is the aftercare or followup program?

Is there a "graduates" group or a concerned parents group that could tell you about the program from the clients' points of view?

On the practical side, what will the program cost and how can treatment be financed?

Eating disorders units or treatment centers now are available in several parts of the country.

Terms to know

amenorrhea. Absence of menstruation.

anorexia nervosa. A condition of self-starvation which affects primarily girls and women between the ages of twelve and thirty, but which can also affect younger and older females as well as males. The "Diagnostic Criteria for Anorexia Nervosa," as listed in the *Diagnostic and Statistical Manual of Mental Disorders* of the American Psychiatric Association (*DSM III*) are as follows:

A. Intense fear of becoming obese, which does not diminish as weight loss progresses.
B. Disturbance of body image, e.g., claiming to "feel fat" even when emaciated.

C. Weight loss of at least 25% of original body weight or, if under 18 years of age, weight loss from original body weight plus projected weight gain expected from growth charts may be combined to make the 25%.
D. Refusal to maintain body weight over a minimal normal weight for age and height.
E. No known physical illness that would account for the weight loss.

anorexic, anorectic. One who has anorexia nervosa (noun), or having anorexia nervosa (adjective). Some researchers prefer "anorectic," but "anorexic" is the word most often used.

arrhythmia. An irregularity in the rhythm of the heartbeat.

body distortion. The unrealistic image anorexics often have of their own bodies; they "feel fat" or see a lie—a fat body—in the mirror. Elke Eckert, M.D., Associate Professor of Psychiatry and Director of the Anorexia Nervosa Treatment Program at University of Minnesota, has developed a body-distortion test to determine how an anorexic perceives her or his own body size.

bulimia. An eating disorder usually associated with young women and characterized by binge-eating, which may be followed by purging—self-induced vomiting or use of laxatives and diuretics. Besides causing chemical imbalances in the body, bulimia is sometimes associated with physical signs such as erosion of tooth enamel, hernia, swollen glands in the neck. The "Diagnostic Criteria for Bulimia" listed in the *DSM III* are as follows:

A. Recurrent episodes of binge eating (rapid consumption of a large amount of food in a discrete period of time, usually less than two hours).
B. At least three of the following:
   1. Consumption of high caloric, easily ingested food during a binge;
   2. Inconspicuous eating during a binge;
   3. Termination of such eating episodes by abdominal pain, sleep, social interruption, or self-induced vomiting;
   4. Repeated attempts to lose weight by severely restrictive diets, self-induced vomiting, or use of cathartics or diuretics;

> 5. Frequent weight fluctuations greater than ten pounds due to alternating binges and fasts;

C. Awareness that the eating pattern is abnormal and fear of not being able to stop eating voluntarily.

D. Depressed mood and self-deprecating thoughts following eating binges.

E. The bulimic episodes are not due to anorexia nervosa or any known physical disorder.

bulimics. Those with the eating disorder of bulimia—a binge-starve or binge-purge syndrome. An estimated 60 to 80 percent of bulimics use self-induced vomiting as the primary method of ridding their bodies of the large quantities of food they consume.

bulimic anorexics. Anorexics with bulimic symptoms, a subgroup of anorexics who alternate between starvation and patterns of bingeing-purging. Although the *DSM III* diagnostic criteria defines anorexia and bulimia as separate problems, the crossover between them has become an area of some controversy. Bulimia in non-emaciated patients usually is considered as a separate syndrome from bulimia in anorexia nervosa. However, many feel that anorexia and bulimia may be phases on a continuum rather than different problems.

caratosis piliaris. The "funny goose bumps" that may develop along with dryness on the skin of a seriously ill anorexic.

diuretic. A substance which reduces body fluids by increasing output of urine.

electrolyte. Chemicals surrounding cell membranes inside and outside which are major forces in controlling fluid balance in the body.

hyperalimentation. Feeding complete nutrition through the veins.

hypothalamus. A hormone-producing gland which regulates many of the body's functions.

lanugo. Fine, downy body hair which sometimes develops with severe anorexia.

primary anorexics. Those who show primary symptoms of anorexia, who control weight primarily through limiting food intake, rather than through bingeing and purging.

Primary anorexics are also called restrictive or restricter anorexics.

Organizations

ANAD—National Association of Anorexia Nervosa and Associated Disorders.
P.O. Box 271, Highland Park, Illinois 60035
(312) 831-3438

ANRED—Anorexia Nervosa and Related Eating Disorders, Inc.
99 West 10th Avenue, Suite 330
Eugene, Oregon 97401
(503) 344-1144

NAAS—National Anorexic Aid Society.
550 S. Cleveland Avenue, Suite F
Westerville, Ohio 43081
(614) 895-2009

BASH—Bulimia Anorexia Self-Help, Inc.
1035 Bellevue Avenue, Suite 104
St. Louis, Missouri 63117
(314) 567-4080 or (314) 991-BASH

American Anorexia/Bulimia Association, Inc.
133 Cedar Lane
Teaneck, New Jersey 07666
(201) 836-1800

Anorexia Nervosa Aid Society of Massachusetts, Inc.
Box 213
Lincoln Center, Massachusetts 01773
(617) 259-9767

Bibliography

American Psychiatric Association. 1980. *Diagnostic and Statistical Manual of Mental Disorders (DSM III)*. Washington, DC: American Psychiatric Association.

Andersen, Arnold E. 1985. *Practical Comprehensive Treatment of Anorexia Nervosa and Bulimia*. Baltimore: Johns Hopkins.

Bray, George A., ed. 1980. *Obesity in America*. Washington, DC: United States Department of Health, Education and Welfare.

Brown, Kim. 1985. When dieting goes berserk. *Parents* magazine. April, 1985.

Bruch, Hilde. 1973. *Eating Disorders: Obesity, Anorexia Nervosa, and the Person Within*. New York: Basic Books, Inc.

———. 1979. *The Golden Cage*. New York: Vintage Books.

Chernin, Kim. 1982. *The Obsession: Reflections on the Tyranny of Slenderness*. New York: Harper Colophon Books.

Crisp, A. H., et al. 1976. How common is anorexia nervosa? A prevalence study. *British Journal of Psychiatry* 128:128.

Feighner, J. P., et al. 1972. Diagnostic criteria for use in psychiatric research. *Archives of General Psychiatry* 26:57.

Garner, David M., and Paul E. Garfinkel. 1985. *Handbook of Psychotherapy for Anorexia Nervosa and Bulimia*. New York: Guilford Press.

Gelbach, Deborah L. 1984. Mirror, mirror. *Twin Cities*. October, 1984.

Halmi, Katherine A., et al. 1981. Binge-eating and vomiting: A survey of a college population. *Psychological Medicine* 11:697.

Hatsukami, Dorothy, et al. 1984. Affective disorders and substance abuse in women with bulimia. *Psychological Medicine* 14.

Huse, Diane M., and Alexander R. Lucas. 1983. Dietary treatment of anorexia nervosa. *Journal of the American Dietetic Association* 83:687.

Keys, Ancel, et al. 1950. *The Biology of Human Starvation*. Minneapolis: University of Minnesota Press.

Nylander, I. 1971. The feeling of being fat and dieting in a schoolgirl population: An epidemiologic interview investigation. *Acta Socio-medica Scandinavica* 3:17.

Orbach, Susie. 1978. *Fat Is a Feminist Issue*. New York: Berkley Publishing Corp.

———. 1982. *Fat Is a Feminist Issue II*. New York: Berkley Publishing Corp.

Patterson, C. H. 1974. *Relationship Counseling and Psychotherapy*. New York: Harper & Row Publishers, Inc.

Rockwell, W. J. Kenneth, et al. 1982. Anorexia nervosa: Review of current treatment practices. *Southern Medical Journal* 75:1101.

Sours, J. A. 1980. *Starving to Death in a Sea of Objects: The Anorexia Nervosa Syndrome*. New York: Jason Aronson.

Strober, Michael. 1983. Subclassification of anorexia nervosa: Psychologic and biologic correlates. In *Understanding Anorexia and Bulimia*, Report of the Fourth Ross Conference on Medical Research. Columbus, Ohio: Ross Laboratories.

Szmukler, George I. 1983. Weight and food preoccupation of English schoolgirls. In *Understanding Anorexia and Bulimia*, Report of the Fourth Ross Conference on Medical Research. Columbus, Ohio: Ross Laboratories.

Vigersky, Robert A., et al. 1976. Anorexia nervosa: behavioural and hypothalamic aspects. *Clinics in Endocrinology and Metabolism* 5:517.

Vigersky, Robert A. 1977. *Anorexia Nervosa*. New York: Raven Press.

Additional reading

Arenson, Gloria. 1984. *Binge-Eating: How to Stop It Forever*. New York: Rawson Associates.

Boskind-White, Marlene and William C. White. 1983. *Bulimarexia: The Binge-Purge Cycle*. New York: Springer Publishing Co., Inc.

Crisp, Arthur H. 1980. *Anorexia Nervosa: Let Me Be*. New York: Grune & Stratton, Inc.

Hawkins, Raymond C. II, et al, eds. 1984. *The Binge-Purge Syndrome: Diagnosis, Treatment, and Research*. New York: Springer Publishing Co., Inc.

Larocca, Felix E. F., ed. 1984. *The Psychiatric Clinics of North America*. No. 7. Philadelphia: W. B. Saunders Co.

Levenkron, Steven. 1978. *The Best Little Girl in the World*. Chicago: Contemporary Books, Inc.

Liu, Aimee. 1979. *Solitaire: A Young Woman's Triumph over Anorexia Nervosa*. New York: Harper Colophon Books.

Minuchin, Salvador, et al. 1978. *Psychosomatic Families: Anorexia Nervosa in Context*. Cambridge: Harvard University Press.

O'Neill, Cherry Boone. 1982. *Starving for Attention*. New York: Dell Publishing Company, Inc.

Roth, Geneen. 1982. *Feeding the Hungry Heart: The Experience of Compulsive Eating*. Indianapolis/New York: The Bobbs-Merrill Company, Inc.

———. 1984. *Breaking Free from Compulsive Eating*. Indianapolis/New York: The Bobbs-Merrill Company, Inc.

About the authors

Patricia M. Stein, R.D., M.S., M.A.

Formerly assistant professor and clinical dietitian in the Outpatient Nutrition Clinic at the University of Kansas College of Health Sciences and Hospital, Patricia Stein is now in private practice in Leawood, Kansas. She specializes in working with individuals who have compulsive overeating and weight management problems, as well as with those recovering from anorexia nervosa and bulimia. She is currently nutrition consultant for the Counseling Institute, Kansas City, Missouri.

She holds two master's degrees—in dietetics from the University of Kansas and in counseling from the University of Missouri, Kansas City.

Author of client education materials and several articles published in newspapers, magazines, and professional journals, she has also been co-editor of the *Kansas Diet Manual*. She is a frequent radio and television guest and a conference speaker on a variety of nutritional and weight management topics. She is a former president of the Kansas City Dietetic Association. Other memberships include the American Dietetic Association, American Association for Counseling and Development, Society of Nutrition Education, Consulting Nutritionists/Registered Dictitians in Private Practice, and the Kansas City Council against Health and Nutrition Fraud and Abuse.

Barbara C. Unell

Barbara Unell is editor of *Twins*, a national bi-monthly magazine for parents of multiples, and publisher of the monthly magazine, *Kansas City Parent*. She is the author of several books, including *The Kansas City Kids Catalog*, and co-author with Jerry Wyckoff, Ph.D. of *Discipline without Shouting or Spanking*.

A graduate of the University of Texas at Austin, she has been a newspaper reporter, a magazine feature writer, and a writer and producer for television. Her many talks around the country on women's issues and family life have included convention presentations for members of state chapters of the National Organization of Mothers of Twins Clubs. She has been a guest on several national radio and television talk shows.